Ava Torre-Bueno

THE MODERN LIBRARY
OF THE WORLD'S BEST BOOKS

THE MOON OF THE CARIBBEES
AND SIX OTHER PLAYS OF THE SEA

*The publishers will be pleased to send, upon re-
quest, an illustrated catalogue setting forth the
purpose and ideals of The Modern Library, and
describing in detail each volume in the series.
❡Every reader of books will find titles he has been
looking for, attractively printed, and
at an unusually low price*

THE MOON OF THE CARIBBEES
AND
SIX OTHER PLAYS OF THE SEA

BY
EUGENE G. O'NEILL

Introduction by
GEORGE JEAN NATHAN

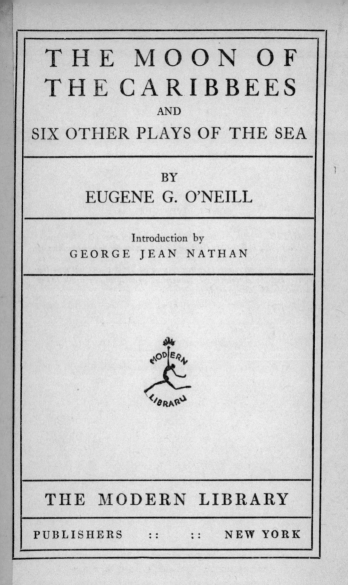

THE MODERN LIBRARY

PUBLISHERS   ::   ::   NEW YORK

MANUFACTURED IN THE UNITED STATES OF AMERICA
FOR THE MODERN LIBRARY, INC., BY H. WOLFF

CONTENTS

INTRODUCTION

In these early short plays, notably in the one called "The Moon of the Caribbees," one detects the first sprigs of a talent that, rapidly coming to flower in succeeding longer plays, is at the present time surely the finest in the American theatre. In O'Neill that theatre has found its first really important dramatist. To it he has brought a sense of splendid colour, a sense of vital drama and a sense of throbbing English that no native playwright before him was able to bring. And with this tripartite sense he has brought, too, an imagination sedulously kept free from those customarily presumed dictates of public taste that have ruined a recognizable number of talented Americans before him.

O'Neill came into the American drama at a propitious moment. His entrance clicked with all the precision and critical timeliness of the entrance of the United States Marines in a piece of popular whangdoodle. Just as this drama seemed about to be laid low by unremitting stereotyped dullness and preposterous affectation, he jumped upon the scene with a bundle of life and fancy under his arm, hurled it onto the stage, and there let it break open with its hundred smashing hues to confound the drab and desolate boards. Instantly—or so it seemed—the stage began to breathe again; instantly the painted backdrop became real and instantly the canvas rocks became solid, substantial. Presently the news of the phenomenon began to spread beyond the little alleys up which O'Neill's plays were forced to find their initial production, and in due time—it was three years, as I remember—it managed to reach even the ears of our recognized producers. But that is now an old story. For today the pre-eminence of O'Neill is taken for granted even by such bizarre æsthetes as in the years before had placed in turn upon the same pedestal Augustus Thomas, Charles Klein, Eugene Walter and Edward Sheldon.

In even the poorer of O'Neill's plays—and he has written poor plays as well as brilliant—one feels a trace of power and bravery. He may on occasion work weakly, but he never works cheaply. Always there is perceptible an effort at something original and distinguished, however far short of the mark that effort may fall. Never is there the suspicion of compromise or of falter. The clearness of the plan is visible, and so is the clearness of the spirit that has sought to put it into execution. What we see is absolute integrity in the process of attempting to achieve itself in terms of drama, and this we see for all the periodic failure of that integrity thus to realize itself.

A play is never finer than the man who creates it. The bulk of the plays of the American theatre are accurate reflections of the shoddy souls and shoddier minds that give, and have given, them being. For one piece of work that affords hint of a craftsman of cultured point of view and traveled imagination we have a score that betray their artificers' ingrained and steadfast commonness. For each Zoë Akins, Jesse Lynch Williams or Tarkington the scene discloses a dozen melancholy clowns at their melancholy antics. For one Eugene O'Neill the same scene discloses half a hundred children, their little diapered talents parading grotesquely and pitiably in the long trousers of maturity. Someone has written—it may have been myself—that when one speaks of the American drama one says O'Neill and is done. While this is not strictly true—for there are other men and women of merit that are happily to be taken into consideration— it is yet not so very far from the truth. For these others are still, with all their merits, in the aggregate but second-raters, while O'Neill and O'Neill alone marches steadily on toward the front line. That line, in the big sense, he has not, of course, yet reached, but he is making progress as no other American playwright is making it. His eyes scan a great world; his ears catch the sardonic counterpoints to the deceptive motifs of human hearts; his ideas smear themselves across canvases of heroic size. In time, it seems certain, his achievements must match fully his capabilities.

The essential difference between O'Neill and the majority of his contemporaries in the field of American drama lies in the circumstance that where the latter think of life (where they think of it at all) in terms of drama, O'Neill thinks of drama in terms of life. Thus, where his contemporaries succeed only in writing the

kind of play that makes of life a mechanical and spirit-
less thing of rubber-stamp exits, entrances, bunch-
lights and drop-curtains, O'Neill succeeds in producing
life itself. The life that he so produces is often not to
the taste of the American audience, for it is not always
a sweet and pretty life—the life which that audience
cherishes across the footlights—but life it is none the
less. It pulses from his stages; it quivers from his
adjectives and verbs. And it makes his manuscripts
warm, beating and vital things. Many American plays
have heart. It has remained for O'Neill, to no little
extent, to add the blood.

GEORGE JEAN NATHAN.

New York, January 1, 1923.

THE MOON OF THE CARIBBEES

A Play In One Act

CHARACTERS

YANK
DRISCOLL
OLSON
DAVIS   *Seamen of the British tramp steamer,*
COCKY   *Glencairn.*
SMITTY
PAUL

LAMPS, *the lamptrimmer.*
CHIPS, *the carpenter.*
OLD TOM, *the donkeyman.*

BIG FRANK
DICK   *Firemen on the Glencairn.*
MAX
PADDY

BELLA
SUSIE   *West Indian Negresses.*
VIOLET
PEARL

THE FIRST MATE
Two other seamen—SCOTTY AND IVAN—and several other members of the stokehole-engine-room crew.

NOTE.—With the exception of "In the Zone," the action of all the plays in this volume takes place in years preceding the outbreak of the World War.

THE MOON OF THE CARIBBEES

Scene—*A forward section of the main deck of the British tramp Steamer* Glencairn, *at anchor off an island in the West Indies. The full moon, half-way up the sky, throws a clear light on the deck. The sea is calm and the ship motionless.*

On the left two of the derrick booms of the foremast jut out at an angle of forty-five degrees, black against the sky. In the rear the dark outline of the port bulwark is sharply defined against a distant strip of coral beach, white in the moonlight, fringed with coco palms whose tops rise clear of the horizon. On the right is the forecastle with an open doorway in the center leading to the seamen's and firemen's compartments. On either side of the doorway are two closed doors opening on the quarters of the Bo'sun, the ship's carpenter, the messroom steward, and the donkeyman— what might be called the petty officers of the ship. Near each bulwark there is also a short stairway, like a section of fire escape, leading up to the forecastle head (the top of the fore-

3

castle)—the edge of which can be seen on the right.

In the center of the deck, and occupying most of the space, is the large, raised square of the number one hatch, covered with canvas, battened down for the night.

A melancholy negro chant, faint and far-off, drifts, crooning, over the water.

Most of the seamen and firemen are reclining or sitting on the hatch. PAUL *is leaning against the port bulwark, the upper part of his stocky figure outlined against the sky.* SMITTY *and* COCKY *are sitting on the edge of the forecastle head with their legs dangling over. Nearly all are smoking pipes or cigarettes. The majority are dressed in patched suits of dungaree. Quite a few are in their bare feet and some of them, especially the firemen, have nothing on but a pair of pants and an undershirt. A good many wear caps.*

There is the low murmur of different conversations going on in the separate groups as the curtain rises. This is followed by a sudden silence in which the singing from the land can be plainly heard.

DRISCOLL—[*A powerfully built Irishman who is sitting on the edge of the hatch, front—irritably.*]

Will ye listen to them naygurs? I wonder now, do they call that keenin' a song?

SMITTY—[*A young Englishman with a blond mustache. He is sitting on the forecastle head looking out over the water with his chin supported on his hands.*] It doesn't make a chap feel very cheerful, does it? [*He sighs.*]

COCKY—[*A wizened runt of a man with a straggling gray mustache—slapping* SMITTY *on the back.*] Cheero, ole dear! Down't be ser dawn in the marf, Duke. She loves yer.

SMITTY—[*Gloomily.*] Shut up, Cocky! [*He turns away from* COCKY *and falls to dreaming again, staring toward the spot on shore where the singing seems to come from.*]

BIG FRANK—[*A huge fireman sprawled out on the right of the hatch—waving a hand toward the land.*] They bury somebody—py chiminy Christmas, I tink so from way it sound.

YANK—[*A rather good-looking rough who is sitting beside* DRISCOLL.] What d'yuh mean, bury? They don't plant 'em down here, Dutchy. They eat 'em to save fun'ral expenses. I guess this guy went down the wrong way an' they got indigestion.

COCKY—Indigestion! Ho yus, not 'arf! Down't yer know as them blokes 'as two stomacks like a bleedin' camel?

DAVIS—[*A short, dark man seated on the right of hatch.*] An' you seen the two, I s'pect, ain't you?

Cocky—[*Scornfully.*] Down't be showin' yer igerance be tryin' to make a mock o' me what has seen more o' the world than yeself ever will.

Max—[*A Swedish fireman—from the rear of hatch.*] Spin dat yarn, Cocky.

Cocky—It's Gawd's troof, what I tole yer. I 'eard it from a bloke what was captured pris'ner by 'em in the Solomon Islands. Shipped wiv 'im one voyage. 'Twas a rare treat to 'ear 'im tell what 'appened to 'im among 'em. [*Musingly.*] 'E was a funny bird, 'e was—'ailed from Mile End, 'e did.

Driscoll—[*With a snort.*] Another lyin' Cockney, the loike av yourself!

Lamps—[*A fat Swede who is sitting on a camp stool in front of his door talking with* Chips.] Where you meet up with him, Cocky?

Chips—[*A lanky Scotchman—derisively.*] In New Guinea, I'll lay my oath!

Cocky—[*Defiantly.*] Yus! It *was* in New Guinea, time I was shipwrecked there. [*There is a perfect storm of groans and laughter at this speech.*]

Yank—[*Getting up.*] Yuh know what we said yuh'd get if yuh sprung any of that lyin' New Guinea dope on us again, don't yuh? Close that trap if yuh don't want a duckin' over the side.

Cocky—Ow, I was on'y tryin' to edicate yer a bit. [*He sinks into dignified silence.*]

Yank—[*Nodding toward the shore.*] Don't yuh

know this is the West Indies, yuh crazy mut? There ain't no cannibals here. They're only common niggers.

DRISCOLL—[*Irritably.*] Whativir they are, the divil take their cryin'. It's enough to give a man the jigs listenin' to 'em.

YANK—[*With a grin.*] What's the matter, Drisc? Yuh're as sore as a boil about somethin'.

DRISCOLL—I'm dyin' wid impatience to have a dhrink; an' that blarsted bumboat naygur woman took her oath she'd bring back rum enough for the lot av us whin she came back on board to-night.

BIG FRANK—[*Overhearing this—in a loud eager voice.*] You say the bumboat voman vill bring booze?

DRISCOLL—[*Sarcastically.*] That's right—tell the Old Man about ut, an' the Mate, too. [*All of the crew have edged nearer to* DRISCOLL *and are listening to the conversation with an air of suppressed excitement.* DRISCOLL *lowers his voice impressively and addresses them all.*] She said she cud snake ut on board in the bottoms av thim baskets av fruit they're goin' to bring wid 'em to sell to us for'ard.

THE DONKEYMAN—[*An old gray-headed man with a kindly, wrinkled face. He is sitting on a camp stool in front of his door, right front.*] She'll be bringin' some black women with her this time—or times has changed since I put in here last.

DRISCOLL—She said she wud—two or three—more, maybe, I dunno. [*This announcement is received with great enthusiasm by all hands.*]

COCKY—Wot a bloody lark!

OLSON—Py yingo, we have one hell of a time!

DRISCOLL—[*Warningly.*] Remimber ye must be quiet about ut, ye scuts—wid the dhrink, I mane—ivin if the bo'sun is ashore. The Old Man ordered her to bring no booze on board or he wudn't buy a thing off av her for the ship.

PADDY—[*A squat, ugly Liverpool Irishman.*] To the divil wid him!

BIG FRANK—[*Turning on him.*] Shud up, you tamn fool, Paddy! You vant make trouble? (*To* DRISCOLL.] You und me, ve keep dem quiet, Drisc.

DRISCOLL—Right ye are, Dutchy. I'll split the skull av the first wan av ye starts to foight. [*Three bells are heard striking.*]

DAVIS—Three bells. When's she comin', Drisc?

DRISCOLL—She'll be here any minute now, surely. [*To* PAUL, *who has returned to his position by the bulwark after hearing* DRISCOLL's *news.*] D'you see 'em comin', Paul?

PAUL—I don't see anyting like bumboat. [*They all set themselves to wait, lighting pipes, cigarettes, and making themselves comfortable. There is a silence broken only by the mournful singing of the negroes on shore.*]

SMITTY—[*Slowly—with a trace of melancholy.*]

I wish they'd stop that song. It makes you think of—well—things you ought to forget. Rummy go, what?

COCKY—[*Slapping him on the back.*] Cheero, ole love! We'll be 'avin our rum in arf a mo', Duke. [*He comes down to the deck, leaving* SMITTY *alone on the forecastle head.*]

BIG FRANK—Sing someting, Drisc. Den ve don't hear dot yelling.

DAVIS—Give us a chanty, Drisc.

PADDY—Wan all av us knows.

MAX—We all sing in on chorus.

OLSON—"Rio Grande," Drisc.

BIG FRANK—No, ve don't know dot. Sing "Viskey Johnny."

CHIPS—"Flyin' Cloud."

COCKY—Now! Guv us "Maid o' Amsterdam."

LAMPS—"Santa Anna" iss good one.

DRISCOLL—Shut your mouths, all av you. [*Scornfully.*] A chanty is ut ye want? I'll bet me whole pay day there's not wan in the crowd 'ceptin' Yank here, an' Ollie, an' meself, an' Lamps an' Cocky, maybe, wud be sailors enough to know the main from the mizzen on a windjammer. Ye've heard the names av chanties but divil a note av the tune or a loine av the words do ye know. There's hardly a rale deep-water sailor lift on the seas, more's the pity.

YANK—Give us "Blow The Man Down." We all

know some of that. [*A chorus of assenting voices:*
Yes!—Righto!—Let 'er drive! Start 'er, Drisc!
etc.]

DRISCOLL—Come in then, all av ye. [*He sings:*]
As I was a-roamin' down Paradise Street—
ALL—Wa-a-ay, blow the man down!
DRISCOLL—As I was a-roamin' down Paradise
Street—
ALL—Give us some time to blow the man down!

CHORUS

Blow the man down, boys, oh, blow
the man down!
Wa-a-ay, blow the man down!
As I was a-roamin' down Paradise
Street—
Give us some time to blow the
man down!

DRISCOLL—A pretty young maiden I chanced **for**
to meet.
ALL—Wa-a-ay, blow the man down!
DRISCOLL—A pretty young maiden I chanced **for**
to meet.
ALL—Give us some time to blow the man down!

CHORUS

Blow the man down, boys, oh, blow
the man down!
Wa-a-ay, blow the man down!

> A pretty young maiden I chanced
>> for to meet.
> Give us some time to blow the
>> man down!

PAUL—[*Just as Driscoll is clearing his throat preparatory to starting the next verse.*] Hay, Drisc! Here she come, I tink. Some bumboat comin' dis way. [*They all rush to the side and look toward the land.*]

YANK—There's five or six of them in it—and they paddle like skirts.

DRISCOLL—[*Wildly elated.*] "Hurroo, ye scuts! 'Tis thim right enough. [*He does a few jig steps on the deck.*]

OLSON—[*After a pause during which all are watching the approaching boat.*] Py yingo, I see six in boat, yes, sir.

DAVIS—I kin make out the baskets. See 'em there amidships?

BIG FRANK—Vot kind booze dey bring—viskey?

DRISCOLL—Rum, foine West Indy rum wid a kick in ut loike a mule's hoind leg.

LAMPS—Maybe she don't bring any; maybe skipper scare her.

DRISCOLL—Don't be throwin' cold water, Lamps. I'll skin her black hoide off av her if she goes back on her worrd.

YANK—Here they come. Listen to 'em gigglin'. [*Calling.*] Oh, you kiddo! [*The sound of women's voices can be heard talking and laughing.*]

DRISCOLL—[*Calling.*]   Is ut you, Mrs. Old Black Joe?

A WOMAN'S VOICE—Ullo, Mike! [*There is loud feminine laughter at this retort.*]

DRISCOLL—Shake a leg an' come abord thin.

THE WOMAN'S VOICE—We're a-comin'.

DRISCOLL—Come on, Yank. You an' me'd best be goin' to give 'em a hand wid their truck. 'Twill put 'em in good spirits.

COCKY—[*As they start off left.*] Ho, you ain't 'arf a fox, Drisc. Down't drink it all afore we sees it.

DRISCOLL—[*Over his shoulder.*] You'll be havin' yours, me sonny bye, don't fret. [*He and Yank go off left.*]

COCKY—[*Licking his lips.*] Gawd blimey, I can do wiv a wet.

DAVIS—Me, too!

CHIPS—I'll bet there ain't none of us'll let any go to waste.

BIG FRANK—I could trink a whole barrel mineself, py chimminy Christmas!

COCKY—I 'opes all the gels ain't as bloomin' ugly as 'er. Looked like a bloody organ-grinder's monkey, she did. Gawd, I couldn't put up wiv the likes of 'er!

PADDY—Ye'll be lucky if any of thim looks at ye, ye squint-eyed runt.

COCKY—[*Angrily.*] Ho, yus? You ain't no bleedin' beauty prize yeself, me man. A 'airy ape, I calls yer.

PADDY—[*Walking toward him—truculently.*] Whot's thot? Say ut again if ye dare.

COCKY—[*His hand on his sheath knife—snarling.*] 'Airy ape! That's wot I says! [PADDY *tries to reach him but the others keep them apart.*]

BIG FRANK—[*Pushing* PADDY *back.*] Vot's the matter mit you, Paddy. Don't you hear vat Driscoll say—no fighting?

PADDY—[*Grumblingly.*] I don't take no back talk from that deck-scrubbin' shrimp.

COCKY—Blarsted coal-puncher! [DRISCOLL *appears wearing a broad grin of satisfaction. The fight is immediately forgotten by the crowd who gather around him with exclamations of eager curiosity.* How is it, Drisc? Any luck? Vot she bring, Drisc? Where's the gels? *etc.*]

DRISCOLL—[*With an apprehensive glance back at the bridge.*] Not so loud, for the love av hivin! [*The clamor dies down.*] Yis, she has ut wid her. She'll be here in a minute wid a pint bottle or two for each wan av ye—three shillin's a bottle. So don't be impashunt.

COCKY—[*Indignantly.*] Three bob! The bloody cow!

SMITTY—[*With an ironic smile.*]   Grand larceny, by God!   [*They all turn and look up at him, surprised to hear him speak.*]

OLSON—Py yingo, we don't pay so much.

BIG FRANK—Tamn black tief!

PADDY—We'll take ut away from her and give her nothin'.

THE CROWD—[*Growling.*]   Dirty thief!   Dot's right!   Give her nothin'!   Not a bloomin' 'apenny! etc.

DRISCOLL—[*Grinning.*]   Ye can take ut or lave ut, me sonny byes.   [*He casts a glance in the direction of the bridge and then reaches inside his shirt and pulls out a pint bottle.*]   'Tis foine rum, the rale stuff.   [*He drinks.*]   I slipped this wan out av wan av the baskets whin they wasn't lookin'.   [*He hands the bottle to* OLSON *who is nearest him.*]   Here ye are, Ollie.   Take a small sup an' pass ut to the nixt.   'Tisn't much but 'twill serve to take the black taste out av your mouths if ye go aisy wid ut.   An' there's buckets more av ut comin'.   [*The bottle passes from hand to hand, each man taking a sip and smacking his lips with a deep "Aaah" of satisfaction.*]

DAVIS—Where's she now, Drisc?

DRISCOLL—Up havin' a worrd wid the skipper, makin' arrangements about the money, I s'pose.

DAVIS—An' where's the other gels?

DRISCOLL—Wid her.   There's foive av thim she

took aboard—two swate little slips av things, near as white as you an' me are, for that gray-whiskered auld fool, an' the mates—an' the engineers too, maybe. The rist av thim'll be comin' for'ard whin she comes.

COCKY—'E ain't 'arf a funny ole bird, the skipper. Gawd blimey! 'Member when we sailed from 'ome 'ow 'e stands on the bridge lookin' like a bloody ole sky pilot? An' 'is missus dawn on the bloomin' dock 'owlin' fit to kill 'erself? An' 'is kids 'owlin' an' wavin' their 'andkerchiefs? [*With great moral indignation.*] An' 'ere 'e is makin' up to a bleedin' nigger! There's a captain for yer! Gawd blimey! Bloody crab, I calls 'im!

DRISCOLL—Shut up, ye insect! Sure, it's not you should be talkin', an' you wid a woman an' childer weepin' for ye in iviry divil's port in the wide worrld, if we can believe your own tale av ut.

COCKY—[*Still indignant.*] I ain't no bloomin' captain, I ain't. I ain't got no missus—reg'lar married, I means. I ain't——

BIG FRANK—[*Putting a huge paw over Cocky's mouth.*] You ain't going talk so much, you hear? [COCKY *wriggles away from him.*] Say, Drisc, how ve pay dis voman for booze? Ve ain't got no cash.

DRISCOLL—It's aisy enough. Each girl'll have a slip av paper wid her an' whin you buy anythin' you write ut down and the price beside ut and sign your name. If ye can't write have some one who can do ut for ye. An' rimimber this: Whin ye buy a bottle av dhrink or [*With a wink.*] somethin' else forbid, ye must write down tobaccy or fruit or somethin' the loike av that. Whin she laves the skipper'll pay what's owin' on the paper an' take ut out av your pay. Is ut clear to ye now?

ALL—Yes—Clear as day—Aw right, Drisc—Righto—Sure. etc.

DRISCOLL—An' don't forgit what I said about bein' quiet wid the dhrink, or the Mate'll be down on our necks an' spile the fun. [*A chorus of assent.*]

DAVIS—[*Looking aft.*] Ain't this them comin'? [*They all look in that direction. The silly laughter of a woman is heard.*]

DRISCOLL—Look at Yank, wud ye, wid his arrm around the middle av wan av thim. That lad's not wastin' any toime. [*The four women enter from the left, giggling and whispering to each other. The first three carry baskets on their heads. The youngest and best-looking comes last. YANK has his arm about her waist and is carrying her basket in his other hand. All four are distinct negro types. They wear light-colored, loose-fitting clothes and have bright bandana handkerchiefs on their heads. They put down their baskets on the hatch and sit down beside them. The men crowd around, grinning.*]

BELLA—[*She is the oldest, stoutest, and homeliest of the four—grinning back at them.*] Ullo, boys.

THE OTHER GIRLS—'Ullo, boys.

THE MEN—Hello, yourself—Evenin'—Hello— How are you? etc.

BELLA—[*Genially.*] Hope you had a nice voyage. My name's Bella, this here's Susie, yander's Violet, and her there [*Pointing to the girl with YANK*] is Pearl. Now we all knows each other.

PADDY—[*Roughly.*] Never mind the girls. Where's the dhrink?

BELLA—[*Tartly.*] You're a hawg, ain't you? Don't talk so loud or you don't git any—you nor no man. Think I wants the ole captain to put me off the ship, do you?"

YANK—Yes, nix on hollerin', you! D'yuh wanta queer all of us?

BELLA—[*Casting a quick glance over her shoulder.*] Here! Some of you big strapping boys sit back of us on the hatch there so's them officers can't see what we're doin'. [*DRISCOLL and several of the others sit and stand in back of the girls on the hatch. BELLA turns to DRISCOLL.*] Did you tell 'em they gotter sign for what they gits—and *how* to sign?

DRISCOLL—I did—what's your name again—oh, yis—Bella, darlin'.

BELLA—Then it's all right; but you boys has gotter go inside the fo'castle when you gits your bottle. No drinkin' out here on deck. I ain't takin' no chances. [*An impatient murmur of assent goes up from the crowd.*] Ain't that right, Mike?

DRISCOLL—Right as rain, darlin'. [BIG FRANK *leans over and says something to him in a low voice.* DRISCOLL *laughs and slaps his thigh.*] Listen, Bella, I've somethin' to ask ye for my little friend here who's bashful. Ut has to do wid the ladies so I'd best be whisperin' ut to ye meself to kape them from blushin. [*He leans over and asks her a question.*]

BELLA—[*Firmly.*] Four shillin's.

DRISCOLL—[*Laughing.*] D'you hear that, all av ye? Four shillin's ut is.

PADDY—[*Angrily.*] To hell wid this talkin'. I want a dhrink.

BELLA—Is everything all right, Mike?

DRISCOLL—[*After a look back at the bridge.*] Sure. Let her droive!

BELLA—All right, girls. [*The girls reach down in their baskets in under the fruit which is on top and each pulls out a pint bottle. Four of the men crowd up and take the bottles.*] Fetch a light, Lamps, that's a good boy. [LAMPS *goes to his room and returns with a candle. This is passed from one girl to another as the men sign the sheets of paper for their bottles.*] Don't you boys forget to mark down cigarettes or tobacco or fruit, re-

member! Three shillin's is the price. Take it into
the fo'castle. For Gawd's sake, don't stand out
here drinkin' in the moonlight. [*The four go into
the forecastle. Four more take their places.* PAD-
DY *plants himself in front of* PEARL *who is sitting
by* YANK *with his arm still around her.*]

PADDY—[*Gruffly.*] Gimme thot! [*She holds
out a bottle which he snatches from her hand. He
turns to go away.*]

YANK—[*Sharply.*] Here, you! Where d'yuh
get that stuff? You ain't signed for that yet.

PADDY—[*Sullenly.*] I can't write me name.

YANK—Then I'll write it for yuh. [*He takes
the paper from Pearl and writes.*] There ain't goin'
to be no welchin' on little Bright Eyes here—not
when I'm around, see? Ain't I right, kiddo?

PEARL—[*With a grin.*] Yes, suh.

BELLA—[*Seeing all four are served.*] Take it
into the fo'castle, boys. [PADDY *defiantly raises
his bottle and gulps down a drink in the full moonlight.* BELLA *sees him.*] Look at 'im! Look at
the dirty swine! [PADDY *slouches into the forecastle.*] Wants to git me in trouble. That settles it! We all got to git inside, boys, where we
won't git caught. Come on, girls. [*The girls
pick up their baskets and follow* BELLA. YANK *and*
PEARL *are the last to reach the doorway. She
lingers behind him, her eyes fixed on* SMITTY, *who is*

still sitting on the forecastle head, his chin on his hands, staring off into vacancy.]

PEARL—[*Waving a hand to attract his attention.*] Come ahn in, pretty boy. Ah likes you.

SMITTY—[*Coldly.*] Yes; I want to buy a bottle, please. [*He goes down the steps and follows her into the forecastle. No one remains on deck but the* DONKEYMAN, *who sits smoking his pipe in front of his door. There is the subdued babble of voices from the crowd inside but the mournful cadence of the song from the shore can again be faintly heard.* SMITTY *reappears and closes the door to the forecastle after him. He shudders and shakes his shoulders as if flinging off something which disgusted him. Then he lifts the bottle which is in his hand to his lips and gulps down a long drink.* THE DONKEYMAN *watches him impassively.* SMITTY *sits down on the hatch facing him. Now that the closed door has shut off nearly all the noise the singing from shore comes clearly over the moonlit water.*]

SMITTY—[*Listening to it for a moment.*] Damn that song of theirs. [*He takes another big drink.*] What do you say, Donk?

THE DONKEYMAN—[*Quietly.*] Seems nice an' sleepy-like.

SMITTY—[*With a hard laugh.*] Sleepy! If I listened to it long—sober—I'd never go to sleep.

THE DONKEYMAN—'Tain't sich bad music, is it?

Sounds kinder pretty to me—low an' mournful—same as listenin' to the organ outside o' church of a Sunday.

SMITTY—[*With a touch of impatience.*] I didn't mean it was bad music. It isn't. It's the beastly memories the damn thing brings up—for some reason. [*He takes another pull at the bottle.*]

THE DONKEYMAN—Ever hear it before?

SMITTY—No; never in my life. It's just a something about the rotten thing which makes me think of—well—oh, the devil! [*He forces a laugh.*]

THE DONKEYMAN—[*Spitting placidly.*] Queer things, mem'ries. I ain't ever been bothered much by 'em.

SMITTY—[Looking *at him fixedly for a moment—with quiet scorn.*] No, you wouldn't be.

THE DONKEYMAN—Not that I ain't had my share o' things goin' wrong; but I puts 'em out o' me mind, like, an' fergets 'em.

SMITTY—But suppose you couldn't put them out of your mind? Suppose they haunted you when you were awake and when you were asleep—what then?

THE DONKEYMAN—[*Quietly.*] I'd git drunk, same's you're doin'.

SMITTY—[*With a harsh laugh.*] Good advice. [*He takes another drink. He is beginning to show the effects of the liquor. His face is flushed and he talks rather wildly.*] We're poor little lambs who have lost our way, eh, Donk? Damned from here to eternity, what? God have mercy on such as we! True, isn't it, Donk?

THE DONKEYMAN—Maybe; I dunno. [*After a slight pause.*] Whatever set you goin' to sea? You ain't made for it.

SMITTY—[*Laughing wildly.*] My old friend in the bottle here, Donk.

THE DONKEYMAN—I done my share o' drinkin' in my time. [*Regretfully.*] Them was good times, those days. Can't hold up under drink no more. Doctor told me I'd got to stop or die. [*He spits contentedly.*] So I stops.

SMITTY—[*With a foolish smile.*] Then I'll drink one for you. Here's your health, old top! [*He drinks.*]

THE DONKEYMAN—[*After a pause.*] S'pose there's a gel mixed up in it someplace, ain't there?

SMITTY—[*Stiffly.*] What makes you think so?

THE DONKEYMAN—Always is when a man lets music bother 'im. [*After a few puffs at his pipe.*] An' she said she threw you over 'cause you was drunk; an' you said you was drunk 'cause she threw you over. [*He spits leisurely.*] Queer thing, love, ain't it?

SMITTY—[*Rising to his feet with drunken dignity.*] I'll trouble you not to pry into my affairs, Donkeyman.

THE DONKEYMAN—[*Unmoved.*] That's every-
body's affair, what I said. I been through it many's
the time. [*Genially.*] I always hit 'em a whack
on the ear an' went out and got drunker'n ever.
When I come home again they always had somethin'
special nice cooked fur me to eat. [*Puffing at his
pipe.*] That's the on'y way to fix 'em when they gits
on their high horse. I don't s'pose you ever tried
that?

SMITTY—[*Pompously.*] Gentlemen don't hit
women.

THE DONKEYMAN—[*Placidly.*] No; that's why
they has mem'ries when they hears music. [*SMITTY
does not deign to reply to this but sinks into a scorn-
ful silence. DAVIS and the girl VIOLET come out of
the forecastle and close the door behind them. He
is staggering a bit and she is laughing shrilly.*]

DAVIS—[*Turning to the left.*] This way, Rose,
or Pansy, or Jessamine, or black Tulip, or Violet,
or whatever the hell flower your name is. No one'll
see us back here. [*They go off left.*]

THE DONKEYMAN—There's love at first sight for
you—an' plenty more o' the same in the fo'c's'tle.
No mem'ries jined with that.

SMITTY—[*Really repelled.*] Shut up, Donk.
You're disgusting. [*He takes a long drink.*]

THE DONKEYMAN—[*Philosophically.*] All de-
pends on how you was brung up, I s'pose.
[*PEARL comes out of the forecastle. There is a*

roar of voices from inside. She shuts the door behind her, sees SMITTY *on the hatch, and comes over and sits beside him and puts her arm over his shoulder.*]

THE DONKEYMAN—[*Chuckling.*] There's love for you, Duke.

PEARL—[*Patting* SMITTY'S *face with her hand.*] 'Ullo, pretty boy. [SMITTY *pushes her hand away coldly.*] What you doin' out here all alone by yourself?

SMITTY—[*With a twisted grin.*] Thinking and,—[*He indicates the bottle in his hand.*]—drinking to stop thinking. [*He drinks and laughs maudlinly. The bottle is three-quarters empty.*]

PEARL—You oughtn't drink so much, pretty boy. Don' you know dat? You have big, big headache come mawnin'.

SMITTY—[*Dryly.*] Indeed?

PEARL—Tha's true. Ah knows what Ah say. [*Cooingly.*] Why you run 'way from me, pretty boy? Ah likes you. Ah don' like them other fellahs. They act too rough. You ain't rough. You're a genelman. Ah knows. Ah can tell a genelman fahs Ah can see 'im.

SMITTY—Thank you for the compliment; but you're wrong, you see. I'm merely—a ranker. [*He adds bitterly.*] And a rotter.

PEARL—[*Patting his arm.*] No, you ain't. Ah knows better. You're a genelman. [*Insinuat-*

ingly.] Ah wouldn't have nothin' to do with them other men, but [*She smiles at him enticingly.*] you is diff'rent. [*He pushes her away from him disgustedly. She pouts.*] Don' you like me, pretty boy?

SMITTY—[*A bit ashamed.*] I beg your pardon. I didn't mean to be rude, you know, really. [*His politeness is drunkenly exaggerated.*] I'm a bit off color.

PEARL—[*Brightening up.*] Den you do like me —little ways?

SMITTY—[*Carelessly.*] Yes, yes, why shouldn't I? [*He suddenly laughs wildly and puts his arm around her waist and presses her to him.*] Why not? [*He pulls his arm back quickly with a shudder of disgust, and takes a drink. PEARL looks at him curiously, puzzled by his strange actions. The door from the forecastle is kicked open and YANK comes out. The uproar of shouting, laughing and singing voices has increased in violence. YANK staggers over toward SMITTY and PEARL.*]

YANK—[*Blinking at them.*] What the hell— oh, it's you, Smitty the Duke. I was goin' to turn one loose on the jaw of any guy'd cop my dame, but seein' it's you—— [*Sentimentally.*] Pals is pals and any pal of mine c'n have anythin' I got, see? [*Holding out his hand.*] Shake, Duke. [*SMITTY takes his hand and he pumps it up and down.*] You'n me's frens. Ain't I right?

SMITTY—Right it is, Yank. But you're wrong about this girl. She isn't with me. She was just going back to the fo'c's'tle to you. [PEARL *looks at him with hatred gathering in her eyes.*]

YANK—Tha' right?

SMITTY—On my word!

YANK—[*Grabbing her arm.*] Come on then, you, Pearl! Le's have a drink with the bunch. [*He pulls her to the entrance where she shakes off his hand long enough to turn on* SMITTY *furiously.*]

PEARL—You swine! You can go to hell! [*She goes in the forecastle, slamming the door.*]

THE DONKEYMAN—[*Spitting calmly.*] There's love for you. They're all the same—white, brown, yeller 'n' black. A whack on the ear's the only thing'll learn 'em. [SMITTY *makes no reply but laughs harshly and takes another drink; then sits staring before him, the almost empty bottle tightly clutched in one hand. There is an increase in volume of the muffled clamor from the forecastle and a moment later the door is thrown open and the whole mob, led by Driscoll, pours out on deck. All of them are very drunk and several of them carry bottles in their hands.* BELLA *is the only one of the women who is absolutely sober. She tries in vain to keep the men quiet.* PEARL *drinks from* YANK'S *bottle every moment or so, laughing shrilly, and leaning against* YANK, *whose arm is about her waist.* PAUL *comes out last carrying an accordion. He staggers over and stands on top of the hatch, his instrument under his arm.*]

DRISCOLL—Play us a dance, ye square-head swab!—a rale, Godforsaken son av a turkey trot wid guts to ut.

YANK—Straight from the old Barbary Coast in Frisco!

PAUL—I don' know. I try. [*He commences tuning up.*]

YANK—Ataboy! Let 'er rip! [DAVIS *and* VIOLET *come back and join the crowd.* THE DONKEYMAN *looks on them all with a detached, indulgent air.* SMITTY *stares before him and does not seem to know there is any one on deck but himself.*]

BIG FRANK—Dance? I don't dance. I trink! [*He suits the action to the word and roars with meaningless laughter.*]

DRISCOLL—Git out av the way thin, ye big hulk, an' give us some room. [BIG FRANK *sits down on the hatch, right. All of the others who are not going to dance either follow his example or lean against the port bulwark.*]

BELLA—[*On the verge of tears at her inability to keep them in the forecastle or make them be quiet now they are out.*] For Gawd's sake, boys, don't shout so loud! Want to git me in trouble?

DRISCOLL—[*Grabbing her.*] Dance wid me, me cannibal quane. [*Some one drops a bottle on deck and it smashes.*]

BELLA—[*Hysterically.*] There they goes! There they goes! Captain'll hear that! Oh, my Lawd!

DRISCOLL—Be damned to him! Here's the music! Off ye go! [PAUL *starts playing "You Great Big Beautiful Doll" with a note left out every now and then. The four couples commence dancing—a jerk-shouldered version of the old Turkey Trot as it was done in the sailor-town dives, made more grotesque by the fact that all the couples are drunk and keep lurching into each other every moment. Two of the men start dancing together, intentionally bumping into the others. YANK and PEARL come around in front of SMITTY and, as they pass him, PEARL slaps him across the side of the face with all her might, and laughs viciously. He jumps to his feet with his fists clenched but sees who hit him and sits down again smiling bitterly. YANK laughs boisterously.*]

YANK—Wow! Some wallop! One on you, Duke.

DRISCOLL—[*Hurling his cap at* PAUL.] Faster, ye toad! [PAUL *makes frantic efforts to speed up and the music suffers in the process.*]

BELLA—[*Puffing.*] Let me go. I'm wore out with you steppin' on my toes, you clumsy Mick. [*She struggles but Driscoll holds her tight.*]

DRISCOLL—God blarst you for havin' such big feet, thin. Aisy, aisy, Mrs. Old Black Joe! 'Tis dancin'll take the blubber off ye. [*He whirls her around the deck by main force.* Cocky, *with* Susie, *is dancing near the hatch, right, when* Paddy, *who is sitting on the edge with* Big Frank, *sticks his foot out and the wavering couple stumble over it and fall flat on the deck. A roar of laughter goes up.* Cocky *rises to his feet, his face livid with rage, and springs at* Paddy, *who promptly knocks him down.* Driscoll *hits* Paddy *and* Big Frank *hits* Driscoll. *In a flash a wholesale fight has broken out and the deck is a surging crowd of drink-maddened men hitting out at each other indiscriminately, although the general idea seems to be a battle between seamen and firemen. The women shriek and take refuge on top of the hatch, where they huddle in a frightened group. Finally there is the flash of a knife held high in the moonlight and a loud yell of pain.*]

Davis—[*Somewhere in the crowd.*] Here's the Mate comin'! Let's git out o' this! [*There is a general rush for the forecastle. In a moment there is no one left on deck but the little group of women on the hatch;* Smitty, *still dazedly rubbing his cheek;* The Donkeyman *quietly smoking on his stool; and* Yank *and* Driscoll, *their faces battered up considerably, their undershirts in shreds, bending over the still form of* Paddy, *which lies stretched out on the deck between them. In the silence the mournful chant from the shore creeps slowly out to the ship.*]

DRISCOLL—[*Quickly—in a low voice.*] Who knoifed him?

YANK—[*Stupidly.*] I didn't see it. How do I know? Cocky, I'll bet. [*The FIRST MATE enters from the left. He is a tall, strongly-built man*

THE MATE—[*Angrily.*] What's all this noise about? [*He sees the man lying on the deck.*] *dressed in a plain blue uniform.*]
Hello! What's this? [*He bends down on one knee beside PADDY.*]

DRISCOLL—[*Stammering.*] All av us—was in a bit av a harmless foight, sir,—an'—I dunno—— [*The MATE rolls PADDY over and sees a knife wound on his shoulder.*]

THE MATE—Knifed, by God. [*He takes an electric flash from his pocket and examines the cut.*] Lucky it's only a flesh wound. He must have hit his head on deck when he fell. That's what knocked him out. This is only a scratch. Take him aft and I'll bandage him up.

DRISCOLL—Yis, sor. [*They take PADDY by the shoulders and feet and carry him off left. The MATE looks up and sees the women on the hatch for the first time.*]

THE MATE—[*Surprised.*] Hello! [*He walks over to them.*] Go to the cabin and get your money and clear off. If I had my way, you'd never—— [*His foot hits a bottle. He stoops down and picks it up and smells of it.*] Rum, by God!

So that's the trouble! I thought their breaths smelled damn queer. [*To the women, harshly.*] You needn't go to the skipper for any money. You won't get any. That'll teach you to smuggle rum on a ship and start a riot.

BELLA—But, Mister——

THE MATE—[*Sternly.*] You know the agreement—rum—no money.

BELLA—[*Indignantly.*] Honest to Gawd, Mister, I never brung no——

THE MATE—[*Fiercely.*] You're a liar! And r.one of your lip or I'll make a complaint ashore tomorrow and have you locked up.

BELLA—[*Subdued.*] Please, Mister—

THE MATE—Clear out of this, now! Not another word out of you! Tumble over the side damn quick! The two others are waiting for you. Hop, now! [*They walk quickly—almost run—off to the left.* THE MATE *follows them, nodding to* THE DONKEYMAN, *and ignoring the oblivious* SMITTY.]

[*There is absolute silence on the ship for a few moments. The melancholy song of the negroes drifts crooning over the water.* SMITTY *listens to it intently for a time; then sighs heavily, a sigh that is half a sob.*]

SMITTY—God! [*He drinks the last drop in the bottle and throws it behind him on the hatch.*]

THE DONKEYMAN—[*Spitting tranquilly.*] More mem'ries? [SMITTY *does not answer him. The ship's bell tolls four bells.* THE DONKEYMAN *knocks out his pipe.*] I think I'll turn in. [*He opens the door to his cabin, but turns to look at* SMITTY— *kindly.*] You can't hear it in the fo'c's'tle—the music, I mean—an' there'll likely be more drink in there, too. Good night. [*He goes in and shuts the door.*]

SMITTY—Good night, Donk. [*He gets wearily to his feet and walks with bowed shoulders, staggering a bit, to the forecastle entrance and goes in. There is silence for a second or so, broken only by the haunted, saddened voice of that brooding music, faint and far-off, like the mood of the moonlight made audible.*]

[*The Curtain Falls*]

BOUND EAST FOR CARDIFF

A Play In One Act

CHARACTERS

Yank

Driscoll

Cocky

Davis

Scotty

Olson

Paul

Smitty

Ivan

The Captain

The Second Mate

BOUND EAST FOR CARDIFF

SCENE—*The seamen's forecastle of the British tramp
steamer* Glencairn *on a foggy night midway on
the voyage between New York and Cardiff.
An irregular shaped compartment, the sides
of which almost meet at the far end to
form a triangle. Sleeping bunks about six feet
long, ranged three deep with a space of three
feet separating the upper from the lower, are
built against the sides. On the right above the
bunks three or four port holes can be seen. In
front of the bunks, rough wooden benches.
Over the bunks on the left, a lamp in a bracket.
In the left foreground, a doorway. On the
floor near it, a pail with a tin dipper. Oilskins
are hanging from a hook near the doorway.*

*The far side of the forecastle is so narrow
that it contains only one series of bunks.*

*In under the bunks a glimpse can be had of
seachests, suit cases, seaboots, etc., jammed in
indiscriminately.*

*At regular intervals of a minute or so the
blast of the steamer's whistle can be heard
above all the other sounds.*

*Five men are sitting on the benches talking.
They are dressed in dirty patched suits of dungaree, flannel shirts, and all are in their stocking feet. Four of the men are pulling on pipes
and the air is heavy with rancid tobacco smoke.
Sitting on the top bunk in the left foreground,
a Norwegian, Paul, is softly playing some folk
song on a battered accordion. He stops from
time to time to listen to the conversation.*

*In the lower bunk in the rear a dark-haired,
hard-featured man is lying apparently asleep.
One of his arms is stretched limply over the side
of the bunk. His face is very pale, and drops
of clammy perspiration glisten on his forehead.*

*It is nearing the end of the dog watch—
about ten minutes to eight in the evening.*

COCKY—[*A weazened runt of a man. He is telling a story. The others are listening with amused,
incredulous faces, interrupting him at the end of
each sentence with loud derisive guffaws.*] Makin'
love to me, she was! It's Gawd's truth! A bloomin'
nigger! Greased all over with cocoanut oil, she
was. Gawd blimey, I couldn't stand 'er. Bloody
old cow, I says; and with that I fetched 'er a biff
on the ear wot knocked 'er silly, an'—— [*He is interrupted by a roar of laughter from the others.*]

DAVIS—[*A middle-aged man with black hair and
mustache.*] You're a liar, Cocky.

SCOTTY—[*A dark young fellow.*]   Ho-ho! Ye
werr neverr in New Guinea in yourr life, I'm thinkin'.

OLSON—[*A Swede with a drooping blond mustache—with ponderous sarcasm.*]   Yust tink of it!
You say she wass a cannibal, Cocky?

DRISCOLL—[*A brawny Irishman with the battered
features of a prizefighter.*]   How cud ye doubt ut,
Ollie? A quane av the naygurs she musta been
surely. Who else wud think herself aqual to fallin'
in love wid a beauthiful, divil-may-care rake av a
man the loike av Cocky? [*A burst of laughter from
the crowd.*]

COCKY—[*Indignantly.*]   Gawd strike me dead if
it ain't true, every bleedin' word of it. 'Appened ten
year ago come Christmas.

SCOTTY—'Twas a Christmas dinner she had her
eyes on.

DAVIS—He'd a been a tough old bird.

DRISCOLL—'Tis lucky for both av ye ye escaped;
for the quane av the cannibal isles wad 'a died av the
belly ache the day afther Christmas, divil a doubt
av ut. [*The laughter at this is long and loud.*]

COCKY—[*Sullenly.*]   Blarsted fat 'eads! [*The
sick man in the lower bunk in the rear groans and
moves restlessly. There is a hushed silence. All
the men turn and stare at him.*]

DRISCOLL—Ssshh! [*In a hushed whisper.*]   We'd
best not be talkin' so loud and him tryin' to have a
bit av a sleep. [*He tiptoes softly to the side of the*

bunk.] Yank! You'd be wantin' a drink av wather, maybe? [YANK *does not reply.* DRISCOLL *bends over and looks at him.*] It's asleep he is, sure enough. His breath is chokin' in his throat loike wather gurglin' in a poipe. [*He comes back quietly and sits down. All are silent, avoiding each other's eyes.*]

COCKY—[*After a pause.*] Pore devil! It's over the side for 'im, Gawd 'elp 'im.

DRISCOLL—Stop your croakin'! He's not dead yet and, praise God, he'll have many a long day yet before him.

SCOTTY—[*Shaking his head doubtfully.*] He's bod, mon, he's verry bod.

DAVIS—Lucky he's alive. Many a man's light woulda gone out after a fall like that.

OLSON—You saw him fall?

DAVIS—Right next to him. He and me was goin' down in number two hold to do some chippin'. He puts his leg over careless-like and misses the ladder and plumps straight down to the bottom. I was scared to look over for a minute, and then I heard him groan and I scuttled down after him. He was hurt bad inside for the blood was drippin' from the side of his mouth. He was groanin' hard, but he never let a word out of him.

COCKY—An' you blokes remember when we 'auled 'im in 'ere? Oh, 'ell, 'e says, oh, 'ell—like that, and nothink else.

OLSON—Did the captain know where he iss hurted?

COCKY—That silly ol' josser! Wot the 'ell would 'e know abaht anythink?

SCOTTY—[*Scornfully.*] He fiddles in his mouth wi' a bit of glass.

DRISCOLL—[*Angrily.*] The divil's own life ut is to be out on the lonely sea wid nothin' betune you and a grave in the ocean but a spindle-shanked, gray-whiskered auld fool the loike av him. 'Twas enough to make a saint shwear to see him wid his gold watch in his hand, tryin' to look as wise as an owl on a tree, and all the toime he not knowin' whether 'twas cholery or the barber's itch was the matther wid Yank.

SCOTTY—[*Sardonically.*] He gave him a dose of salts, na doot?

DRISCOLL—Divil a thing he gave him at all, but looked in the book he had wid him, and shook his head, and walked out widout sayin' a word, the second mate afther him no wiser than himself, God's curse on the two av thim!

COCKY—[*After a pause.*] Yank was a good shipmate, pore beggar. Lend me four bob in Noo Yark, 'e did.

DRISCOLL—[*Warmly.*] A good shipmate he was and is, none betther. Ye said no more than the truth, Cocky. Five years and more ut is since first I shipped wid him, and we've stuck together iver since through good luck and bad. Fights we've had, God help us, but 'twas only when we'd a bit av drink taken, and we always shook hands the nixt mornin'. Whativer was his was mine, and many's the toime I'd a been on the beach or worse, but for him. And now—— [*His voice trembles as he fights to control his emotion.*] Divil take me if I'm not startin' to blubber loike an auld woman, and he not dead at all, but goin' to live many a long year yet, maybe.

DAVIS—The sleep'll do him good. He seems better now.

OLSON—If he wude eat someting——

DRISCOLL—Wud ye have him be eatin' in his condishun? Sure it's hard enough on the rest av us wid nothin' the matther wid our insides to be stomachin' the skoff on this rusty lime-juicer.

SCOTTY—[*Indignantly.*] It's a starvation ship.

DAVIS—Plenty o' work and no food—and the owners ridin' around in carriages!

OLSON—Hash, hash! Stew, stew! Marmalade, py damn! [*He spits disgustedly.*]

COCKY—Bloody swill! Fit only for swine is wot I say.

DRISCOLL—And the dishwather they disguise wid the name av tea! And the putty they call bread! My belly feels loike I'd swalleyed a dozen rivets at the thought av ut! And sea-biscuit that'd break the teeth av a lion if he had the misfortune to take a bite at one! [*Unconsciously they have all raised their voices, forgetting the sick man in their sailor's delight at finding something to grumble about.*]

PAUL—[*Swings his feet over the side of his bunk, stops playing his accordion, and says slowly*]: And rot-ten po-tay-toes! [*He starts in playing again. The sick man gives a groan of pain.*]

DRISCOLL—[*Holding up his hand.*] Shut your mouths, all av you. 'Tis a hell av a thing for us to be complainin' about our guts, and a sick man maybe dyin' listenin' to us. [*Gets up and shakes his fist at the Norwegian.*] God stiffen you, ye square-head scut! Put down that organ av yours or I'll break your ugly face for you. Is that banshee schreechin' fit music for a sick man? [*The Norwegian puts his accordion in the bunk and lies back and closes his eyes. DRISCOLL goes over and stands beside YANK. The steamer's whistle sounds particularly loud in the silence.*]

DAVIS—Damn this fog! [*Reaches in under a bunk and yanks out a pair of seaboots, which he pulls on.*] My lookout next, too. Must be nearly eight bells, boys. [*With the exception of OLSON, all the men sitting up put on oilskins, sou'westers, sea-boots, etc., in preparation for the watch on deck. Olson crawls into a lower bunk on the right.*]

SCOTTY—My wheel.

OLSON—[*Disgustedly.*] Nothin' but yust dirty weather all dis voyage. I yust can't sleep when weestle blow. [*He turns his back to the light and is soon fast asleep and snoring.*]

SCOTTY—If this fog keeps up, I'm tellin' ye, we'll no be in Carrdiff for a week or more.

DRISCOLL—'Twas just such a night as this the auld Dover wint down. Just about this toime ut was, too, and we all sittin' round in the fo'castle, Yank beside me, whin all av a suddint we heard a great slitherin' crash, and the ship heeled over till we was all in a heap on wan side. What came afther I disremimber exactly, except 'twas a hard shift to get the boats over the side before the auld teakittle sank. Yank was in the same boat wid me, and sivin morthal days we drifted wid scarcely a drop of wather or a bite to chew on. 'Twas Yank here that held me down whin I wanted to jump into the ocean, roarin' mad wid the thirst. Picked up we were on the same day wid only Yank in his senses, and him steerin' the boat.

COCKY—[*Protestingly.*] Blimey but you're a cheerful blighter, Driscoll! Talkin' abaht ship-wrecks in this 'ere blushin' fog. [YANK *groans and stirs uneasily, opening his eyes.* DRISCOLL *hurries to his side.*]

DRISCOLL—Are ye feelin' any betther, Yank?

YANK—[*In a weak voice.*] No.

DRISCOLL—Sure, you must be. You look as sthrong as an ox. [*Appealing to the others.*] Am I tellin' him a lie?

DAVIS—The sleep's done you good.

COCKY—You'll be 'avin your pint of beer in Cardiff this day week.

SCOTTY—And fish and chips, mon!

YANK—[*Peevishly.*] What're yuh all lyin' fur? D'yuh think I'm scared to—— [*He hesitates as if frightened by the word he is about to say.*]

DRISCOLL—Don't be thinkin' such things! [*The ship's bell is heard heavily tolling eight times. From the forecastle head above the voice of the lookout rises in a long wail: Aaall's welll. The men look uncertainly at* YANK *as if undecided whether to say good-by or not.*]

YANK—[*In an agony of fear.*] Don't leave me, DRISC! I'm dyin', I tell yuh. I won't stay here alone with every one snorin'. I'll go out on deck. [*He makes a feeble attempt to rise, but sinks back with a sharp groan. His breath comes in wheezy gasps.*] Don't leave me, Drisc! [*His face grows white and his head falls back with a jerk.*]

DRISCOLL—Don't be worryin', Yank. I'll not move a step out av here—and let that divil av a bosun curse his black head off. You speak a word to the bosun, Cocky. Tell him that Yank is bad took and I'll be stayin' wid him a while yet.

COCKY—Right-o. [COCKY, DAVIS, *and* SCOTTY *go out quietly.*]

COCKY—[*From the alleyway.*] Gawd blimey, the fog's thick as soup.

DRISCOLL—Are ye satisfied now, Yank? [*Receiving no answer, he bends over the still form.*] He's fainted, God help him! [*He gets a tin dipper from the bucket and bathes YANK's forehead with the water. YANK shudders and opens his eyes.*]

YANK—[*Slowly.*] I thought I was goin' then. Wha' did yuh wanta wake me up fur?

DRISCOLL—[*With forced gayety.*] Is it wishful for heaven ye are?

YANK—[*Gloomily.*] Hell, I guess.

DRISCOLL—[*Crossing himself involuntarily.*] For the love av the saints don't be talkin' loike that! You'd give a man the creeps. It's chippin' rust on deck you'll be in a day or two wid the best av us. [*YANK does not answer, but closes his eyes wearily. The seaman who has been on lookout, SMITTY, a young Englishman, comes in and takes off his dripping oilskins. While he is doing this the man whose turn at the wheel has been relieved enters. He is a dark burly fellow with a round stupid face. The Englishman steps softly over to DRISCOLL. The other crawls into a lower bunk.*]

SMITTY—[*Whispering.*] How's Yank?

DRISCOLL—Betther. Ask him yourself. He's awake.

YANK—I'm all right, Smitty.

SMITTY—Glad to hear it, Yank. [*He crawls to an upper bunk and is soon asleep.*]

IVAN—[*The stupid-faced seaman who came in af-*

ter SMITTY *twists his head in the direction of the sick man.*] You feel gude, Jank?

YANK—[*Wearily.*] Yes, Ivan.

IVAN—Dot's gude. [*He rolls over on his side and falls asleep immediately.*]

YANK—[*After a pause broken only by snores—with a bitter laugh.*] Good-by and good luck to the lot of you!

DRISCOLL—Is ut painin' you again?

YANK—It hurts like hell—here. [*He points to the lower part of his chest on the left side.*] I guess my old pump's busted. Ooohh! [*A spasm of pain contracts his pale features. He presses his hand to his side and writhes on the thin mattress of his bunk. The perspiration stands out in beads on his forehead.*]

DRISCOLL—[*Terrified.*] Yank! Yank! What is ut? [*Jumping to his feet.*] I'll run for the captain. [*He starts for the doorway.*]

YANK—[*Sitting up in his bunk, frantic with fear.*] Don't leave me, Drisc! For God's sake don't leave me alone! [*He leans over the side of his bunk and spits.* DRISCOLL *comes back to him.*] Blood! Ugh!

DRISCOLL—Blood again! I'd best be gettin' the captain.

YANK—No, no, don't leave me! If yuh do I'll git up and follow you. I ain't no coward, but I'm scared to stay here with all of them asleep and snorin'. [DRISCOLL, *not knowing what to do, sits down on the bench beside him. He grows calmer and sinks back on the mattress.*] The captain can't do me no good, yuh know it yourself. The pain ain't so bad now, but I thought it had me then. It was like a buzz-saw cuttin' into me.

DRISCOLL—[*Fiercely.*] God blarst ut!

[*The captain and the second mate of the steamer enter the forecastle. The captain is an old man with gray mustache and whiskers. The mate is clean-shaven and middle-aged. Both are dressed in simple blue uniforms.*]

THE CAPTAIN—[*Taking out his watch and feeling* YANK's *pulse.*] And how is the sick man?

YANK—[*Feebly.*] All right, sir.

THE CAPTAIN—And the pain in the chest?

YANK—It still hurts, sir, worse than ever.

THE CAPTAIN—[*Taking a thermometer from his pocket and putting it into* YANK's *mouth.*] Here. Be sure and keep this in under your tongue, not over it.

THE MATE—[*After a pause.*] Isn't this your watch on deck, DRISCOLL?

DRISCOLL—Yes, sorr, but Yank was fearin' to be alone, and——

THE CAPTAIN—That's all right, Driscoll.

DRISCOLL—Thank ye, sorr.

THE CAPTAIN—[*Stares at his watch for a moment or so; then takes the thermometer from* YANK's *mouth and goes to the lamp to read it. His expression grows very grave. He beckons the* MATE *and* DRISCOLL *to the corner near the doorway.* YANK *watches them furtively. The* CAPTAIN *speaks in a low voice to the* MATE.] Way up, both of them. [*To* DRISCOLL]: Has he been spitting blood **again**?

DRISCOLL—Not much for the hour just past, sorr, but before that——

THE CAPTAIN—A great deal?

DRISCOLL—Yes, sorr.

THE CAPTAIN—He hasn't eaten anything?

DRISCOLL—No, sorr.

THE CAPTAIN—Did he drink that medicine I sent him?

DRISCOLL—Yes, sorr, but it didn't stay down.

THE CAPTAIN—[*Shaking his head.*] I'm afraid —he's very weak. I can't do anything else for him. It's too serious for me. If this had only happened a week later we'd be in Cardiff in time to——

DRISCOLL—Plaze help him some way, sorr!

THE CAPTAIN—[*Impatiently.*] But, my good man, I'm not a doctor. [*More kindly as he sees* DRISCOLL'*s grief.*] You and he have been shipmates a long time?

DRISCOLL—Five years and more, sorr.

THE CAPTAIN—I see. Well, don't let him move. Keep him quiet and we'll hope for the best. I'll read the matter up and send him some medicine, something to ease the pain, anyway. [*Goes over to*

YANK.] Keep up your courage! You'll be better to-morrow. [*He breaks down lamely before* YANK's *steady gaze.*] We'll pull you through all right— and—hm—well—coming, Robinson? Dammit! [*He goes out hurriedly, followed by the* MATE.]

DRISCOLL—[*Trying to conceal his anxiety.*] Didn't I tell you you wasn't half as sick as you thought you was? The Captain'll have you out on deck cursin' and swearin' loike a trooper before the week is out.

YANK—Don't lie, DRISC. I heard what he said, and if I didn't I c'd tell by the way I feel. I know what's goin' to happen. I'm goin' to—— [*He hesitates for a second—then resolutely.*] I'm goin' to die, that's what, and the sooner the better!

DRISCOLL—[*Wildly.*] No, and be damned to you, you're not. I'll not let you.

YANK—It ain't no use, Drisc. I ain't got a chance, but I ain't scared. Gimme a drink of water, will yuh, Drisc? My throat's burnin' up. [DRIS-COLL *brings the dipper full of water and supports his head while he drinks in great gulps.*]

DRISCOLL—[*Seeking vainly for some word of comfort.*] Are ye feelin' more aisy loike now?

YANK—Yes—now—when I know it's all up. [*A pause.*] You must'nt take it so hard, Drisc. I was just thinkin' it ain't as bad as people think— dyin'. I ain't never took much stock in the truck them sky-pilots preach. I ain't never had religion;

but I know whatever it is what comes after it can't be no worser'n this. I don't like to leave you, Drisc, but—that's all.

DRISCOLL—[*With a groan.*] Lad, lad, don't be talkin'.

YANK—This sailor life ain't much to cry about leavin'—just one ship after another, hard work, small pay, and bum grub; and when we git into port, just a drunk endin' up in a fight, and all your money gone, and then ship away again. Never meetin' no nice people; never gittin outa sailor town, hardly, in any port; travellin' all over the world and never seein' none of it; without no one to care whether you're alive or dead. [*With a bitter smile.*] There ain't much in all that that'd make yuh sorry to lose it, Drisc.

DRISCOLL—[*Gloomily.*] It's a hell av a life, the sea.

YANK—[*Musingly.*] It must be great to stay on dry land all your life and have a farm with a house of your own with cows and pigs and chickens, 'way in the middle of the land where yuh'd never smell the sea or see a ship. It must be great to have a wife, and kids to play with at night after supper when your work was done. It must be great to have a home of your own, Drisc.

DRISCOLL—[*With a great sigh.*] It must, surely; but what's the use av thinkin' av ut? Such things are not for the loikes av us.

YANK—Sea-farin' is all right when you're young and don't care, but we ain't chickens no more, and somehow, I dunno, this last year has seemed rotten, and I've had a hunch I'd quit—with you, of course —and we'd save our coin, and go to Canada or Argentine or some place and git a farm, just a small one, just enough to live on. I never told yuh this cause I thought you'd laugh at me.

DRISCOLL—[*Enthusiastically.*] Laugh at you, is ut? When I'm havin' the same thoughts myself, toime afther toime. It's a grand idea and we'll be doin' ut sure if you'll stop your crazy notions— about—about bein' so sick.

YANK—[*Sadly.*] Too late. We shouldn'ta made this trip, and then—— How'd all the fog git in here?

DRISCOLL—Fog?

YANK—Everything looks misty. Must be my eyes gittin' weak, I guess. What was we talkin' of a minute ago? Oh, yes, a farm. It's too late. [*His mind wandering.*] Argentine, did I say? D'yuh remember the times we've had in Buenos Aires? The moving pictures in Barracas? Some class to them, d'yuh remember?

DRISCOLL—[*With satisfaction.*] I do that; and so does the piany player. He'll not be forgettin' the black eye I gave him in a hurry.

YANK—Remember the time we was there on the beach and had to go to Tommy Moore's boarding house to git shipped? And he sold us rotten oil-skins and seaboots full of holes, and shipped us on a skysail yarder round the Horn, and took two months' pay for it. And the days we used to sit on the park benches along the Paseo Colon with the vigilantes lookin' hard at us? And the songs at the Sailor's Opera where the guy played ragtime—d'yuh remember them?

DRISCOLL—I do, surely.

YANK—And La Plata—phew, the stink of the hides! I always liked Argentine—all except that booze, caña. How drunk we used to git on that, remember?

DRISCOLL—Cud I forget ut? My head pains me at the menshun av that divil's brew.

YANK—Remember the night I went crazy with the heat in Singapore? And the time you was pinched by the cops in Port Said? And the time we was both locked up in Sydney for fightin'?

DRISCOLL—I do so.

YANK—And that fight on the dock at Cape Town——[*His voice betrays great inward perturbation.*]

DRISCOLL—[*Hastily.*] Don't be thinkin' av that now. 'Tis past and gone.

YANK—D'yuh think He'll hold it up against me?

DRISCOLL—[*Mystified.*] Who's that?

YANK—God. They say He sees everything. He

must know it was done in fair fight, in self-defense,
don't yuh think?

DRISCOLL—Av course. Ye stabbed him, and be
damned to him, for the skulkin' swine he was, afther
him tryin' to stick you in the back, and you not
suspectin'. Let your conscience be aisy. I wisht
I had nothin' blacker than that on my sowl. I'd not
be afraid av the angel Gabriel himself.

YANK—[*With a shudder.*] I c'd see him a minute
ago with the blood spurtin' out of his neck. Ugh!

DRISCOLL—The fever, ut is, that makes you see
such things. Give no heed to ut.

YANK—[*Uncertainly.*] You don't think He'll
hold it up agin me—God, I mean.

DRISCOLL—If there's justice in hiven, no! [YANK
seems comforted by this assurance.]

YANK—[*After a pause.*] We won't reach Cardiff for a week at least. I'll be buried at sea.

DRISCOLL—[*Putting his hands over his ears.*]
Ssshh! I won't listen to you.

YANK—[*As if he had not heard him.*] It's as
good a place as any other, I s'pose—only I always
wanted to be buried on dry land. But what the
hell'll I care—then? [*Fretfully.*] Why should it
be a rotten night like this with that damned whistle
blowin' and people snorin' all round? I wish the
stars was out, and the moon, too; I c'd lie out on
deck and look at them, and it'd make it easier to go
—somehow.

DRISCOLL—For the love av God don't be talkin' loike that!

YANK—Whatever pay's comin' to me yuh can divvy up with the rest of the boys; and you take my watch. It ain't worth much, but it's all I've got.

DRISCOLL—But have ye no relations at all to call your own?

YANK—No, not as I know of. One thing I forgot: You know Fanny the barmaid at the Red Stork in Cardiff?

DRISCOLL—Sure, and who doesn't?

YANK—She's been good to me. She tried to lend me half a crown when I was broke there last trip. Buy her the biggest box of candy yuh c'n find in Cardiff. [*Breaking down—in a choking voice.*] It's hard to ship on this voyage I'm goin' on—alone! [DRISCOLL *reaches out and grasps his hand. There is a pause, during which both fight to control themselves.*] My throat's like a furnace. [*He gasps for air.*] Gimme a drink of water, will yuh, Drisc? [DRISCOLL *gets him a dipper of water.*] I wish this was a pint of beer. Oooohh! [*He chokes, his face convulsed with agony, his hands tearing at his shirt front. The dipper falls from his nerveless fingers.*]

DRISCOLL—For the love av God, what is ut, Yank?

YANK—[*Speaking with tremendous difficulty.*] S'long, Drisc! [*He stares straight in front of him with eyes starting from their sockets.*] Who's that?

DRISCOLL—Who? What?

YANK—[*Faintly.*]   A pretty lady dressed in black. [*His face twitches and his body writhes in a final spasm, then straightens out rigidly.*]

DRISCOLL—[*Pale with horror.*]   Yank! Yank! Say a word to me for the love av hiven! [*He shrinks away from the bunk, making the sign of the cross. Then comes back and puts a trembling hand on* YANK's *chest and bends closely over the body.*]

COCKY—[*From the alleyway.*]   Oh, Driscoll! Can you leave Yank for arf a mo' and give me a 'and?

DRISCOLL—[*With a great sob.*]   Yank! [*He sinks down on his knees beside the bunk, his head on his hands. His lips move in some half-remembered prayer.*]

COCKY—[*Enters, his oilskins and sou'wester glistening with drops of water.*]   The fog's lifted. [COCKY *sees* DRISCOLL *and stands staring at him with open mouth.* DRISCOLL *makes the sign of the cross again.*]

COCKY—[*Mockingly.*]   Sayin' 'is prayers! [*He catches sight of the still figure in the bunk and an expression of awed understanding comes over his face. He takes off his dripping sou'wester and stands, scratching his head.*]

COCKY—[*In a hushed whisper.*]   Gawd blimey!

[*The Curtain Falls*]

THE LONG VOYAGE HOME

A Play In One Act

CHARACTERS

FAT JOE, *proprietor of a dive.*

NICK, *a crimp.*

MAG, *a barmaid.*

OLSON

DRISCOLL } *Seamen of the British tramp steamer.*

COCKY *Glencairn.*

IVAN

KATE

FREDA

TWO ROUGHS

THE LONG VOYAGE HOME

SCENE—*The bar of a low dive on the London water front—a squalid, dingy room dimly lighted by kerosene lamps placed in brackets on the walls. On the left, the bar. In front of it, a door leading to a side room. On the right, tables with chairs around them. In the rear, a door leading to the street.*

A slovenly barmaid with a stupid face sodden with drink is mopping off the bar. Her arm moves back and forth mechanically and her eyes are half shut as if she were dozing on her feet. At the far end of the bar stands FAT JOE, the proprietor, a gross bulk of a man with an enormous stomach. His face is red and bloated, his little piggish eyes being almost concealed by rolls of fat. The thick fingers of his big hands are loaded with cheap rings and a gold watch chain of cable-like proportions stretches across his checked waistcoat.

At one of the tables, front, a round-shouldered young fellow is sitting, smoking a cigarette. His face is pasty, his mouth weak, his eyes shifting and cruel. He is dressed in a shabby suit, which must have once been cheaply flashy, and wears a muffler and cap.

It is about nine o'clock in the evening.

JOE—[*Yawning.*] Blimey if bizness ain't 'arf slow to-night. I donnow wot's 'appened. The place is like a bleedin' tomb. Where's all the sailor men, I'd like to know? [*Raising his voice.*] Ho, you Nick! [NICK *turns around listlessly.*] Wot's the name o' that wessel put in at the dock below jest arter noon?

NICK—[*Laconically.*] Glencairn—from Bewnezerry. (Buenos Aires).

JOE—Ain't the crew been paid orf yet?

NICK—Paid orf this arternoon, they tole me. I 'opped on board of 'er an' seen 'em. 'Anded 'em some o' yer cards, I did. They promised faithful they'd 'appen in to-night—them as whose time was done.

JOE—Any two-year men to be paid orf?

NICK—Four—three Britishers an' a square-'ead.

JOE—[*Indignantly.*] An' yer popped orf an' left 'em? An' me a-payin' yer to 'elp an' bring 'em in 'ere!

NICK—[*Grumblingly.*] Much you pays me! An' I ain't slingin' me 'ook abaht the 'ole bleedin' town fur now man. See?

JOE—I ain't speakin' on'y fur meself. Down't

I always give yer yer share, fair an' square, as man to man?

NICK—[*With a sneer.*] Yus—b'cause you 'as to.

JOE—'As to? Listen to 'im! There's many'd be 'appy to 'ave your berth, me man!

NICK—Yus? Wot wiv the peelers li'ble to put me away in the bloody jail fur crimpin', an' all?

JOE—[*Indignantly.*] We down't do no crimpin'.

NICK—[*Sarcastically.*] Ho, now! Not arf!

JOE—[*A bit embarrassed.*] Well, on'y a bit now an' agen when there ain't no reg'lar trade. [*To hide his confusion he turns to the barmaid angrily. She is still mopping off the bar, her chin on her breast, half-asleep.*] 'Ere, me gel, we've 'ad enough o' that. You been a-moppin', an' a-moppin', an' a-moppin' the blarsted bar fur a 'ole 'our. 'Op it aht o' this! You'd fair guv a bloke the shakes a-watchin' yer.

MAG—[*Beginning to sniffle.*] Ow, you do frighten me when you 'oller at me, Joe. I ain't a bad gel, I ain't. Gawd knows I tries to do me best fur you. [*She bursts into a tempest of sobs.*]

JOE—[*Roughly.*] Stop yer grizzlin'! An' 'op it aht of 'ere!

NICK—[*Chuckling.*] She's drunk, Joe. Been 'ittin' the gin, eh, Mag?

MAG—[*Ceases crying at once and turns on him furiously.*] You little crab, you! Orter wear a muzzle, you ort! A-openin' of your ugly mouth to a 'onest woman what ain't never done you no 'arm.

[*Commencing to sob again.*] H'abusin' me like a dawg cos I'm sick an' orf me oats, an' all.

Joe—Orf yer go, me gel! Go hupstairs and 'ave a sleep. I'll wake yer if I wants yer. An' wake the two gels when yer goes hup. It's 'arpas' nine an' time as some one was a-comin' in, tell 'em. D'yer 'ear me?

Mag—[*Stumbling around the bar to the door on left—sobbing.*] Yus, yus, I 'ears you. Gawd knows wot's goin' to 'appen to me, I'm that sick. Much you cares if I dies, down't you? [*She goes out.*]

Joe—[*Still brooding over* Nick's *lack of diligence—after a pause.*] Four two-year men paid orf wiv their bloody pockets full o' sovereigns—an' yer lorst 'em. [*He shakes his head sorrowfully.*]

Nick—[*Impatiently.*] Stow it! They promised faithful they'd come, I tells yer. They'll be walkin' in in 'arf a mo'. There's lots o' time yet. [*In a low voice.*] 'Ave yer got the drops? We might wanter use 'em.

Joe—[*Taking a small bottle from behind the bar.*] Yus; 'ere it is.

Nick—[*With satisfaction.*] Righto! [*His shifty eyes peer about the room searchingly. Then he beckons to* Joe, *who comes over to the table and sits down.*] Reason I arst yer about the drops was 'cause I seen the capt'n of the Amindra this arternoon.

Joe—The Amindra? Wot ship is that?

NICK—Bloody windjammer—skys'l yarder—full rigged—painted white—been layin' at the dock above 'ere fur a month. You knows 'er.

JOE—Ho, yus. I knows now.

NICK—The capt'n says as 'e wants a man special bad—ter-night. They sails at daybreak ter-morrer.

JOE—There's plenty o' 'ands lyin' abaht waitin' fur ships, I should fink.

NICK—Not fur this ship, ole buck. The capt'n an' mate are bloody slave-drivers, an' they're bound down round the 'Orn. They 'arf starved the 'ands on the larst trip 'ere, an' no one'll dare ship on 'er. [After a pause.] I promised the capt'n faithful I'd get 'im one, and ter-night.

JOE—[Doubtfully.] An' 'ow are yer goin' to git 'im?

NICK—[With a wink.] I was thinkin' as one of 'em from the Glencairn'd do—them as was paid orf an' is comin' 'ere.

JOE—[With a grin.] It'd be a good 'aul, that's the troof. [Frowning.] If they comes 'ere.

NICK—They'll come, an' they'll all be rotten drunk, wait an' see. [There is the noise of loud, boisterous singing from the street.] Sounds like 'em, now. [He opens the street door and looks out.] Gawd blimey if it ain't the four of 'em! [Turning to Joe in triumph.] Naw, what d'yer say? They're lookin' for the place. I'll go aht an' tell 'em. [He *goes out. Joe gets into position behind the bar, assuming his most oily smile. A moment later the door is opened, admitting* DRISCOLL, COCKY, IVAN *and* OLSON. DRISCOLL *is a tall, powerful Irishman;* COCKY, *a wizened runt of a man with a straggling gray mustache;* IVAN, *a hulking oaf of a peasant;* OLSON, *a stocky, middle-aged Swede with round, childish blue eyes. The first three are all very drunk, especially* IVAN, *who is managing his legs with difficulty.* OLSON *is perfectly sober. All are dressed in their ill-fitting shore clothes and look very uncomfortable.* DRISCOLL *has unbuttoned his stiff collar and its ends stick out sideways. He has lost his tie.* NICK *slinks into the room after them and sits down at a table in rear. The seamen come to the table, front.*]

JOE—[*With affected heartiness.*] Ship ahoy, mates! 'Appy to see yer 'ome safe an' sound.

DRISCOLL—[*Turns round, swaying a bit, and peers at him across the bar.*] So ut's you, is ut? [*He looks about the place with an air of recognition.*] 'An the same damn rat's-hole, sure enough. I remimber foive or six years back 'twas here I was sthripped av me last shillin' whin I was aslape. [*With sudden fury.*] God stiffen ye, come none av your dog's thricks on me this trip or I'll—— [*He shakes his fist at* JOE.]

JOE—[*Hastily interrupting.*] Yer must be mistaiken. This is a 'onest place, this is.

COCKY—[*Derisively.*]   Ho, yus!   An' you're a bleedin' angel, I s'pose?

IVAN—[*Vaguely taking off his derby hat and putting it on again—plaintively.*]   I don' li-ike dis place.

DRISCOLL—[*Going over to the bar—as genial as he was furious a moment before.*]   Well, no matther, 'tis all past an' gone an' forgot.   I'm not the man to be holdin' harrd feelin's on me first night ashore, an' me dhrunk as a lord.   [*He holds out his hand, which* JOE *takes very gingerly.*]   We'll all be havin' a dhrink, I'm thinkin'.   Whiskey for the three av us—*Irish* whiskey!

COCKY—[*Mockingly.*]   An' a glarse o' ginger beer fur our blarsted love-child 'ere.   [*He jerks his thumb at* OLSON.]

OLSON—[*With a good-natured grin.*]   I bane a good boy dis night, for one time.

DRISCOLL—[*Bellowing, and pointing to* NICK *as* JOE *brings the drinks to the table.*]   An' see what that crimpin' son av a crimp'll be wantin'—an' have your own pleasure.   [*He pulls a sovereign out of his pocket and slams it on the bar.*]

NICK—Guv me a pint o' beer, Joe.   [JOE *draws the beer and takes it down to the far end of the bar.* NICK *comes over to get it and* JOE *gives him a significant wink and nods toward the door on the left.* NICK *signals back that he understands.*]

COCKY—[*Drink in hand—impatiently.*]   I'm that

bloody dry! [*Lifting his glass to* DRISCOLL.] Cheero, ole dear, cheero!

DRISCOLL—[*Pocketing his change without looking at it.*] A toast for ye: Hell roast that divil av a bo'sun! [*He drinks.*]

COCKY—Righto! Gawd strike 'im blind! [*He drains his glass.*]

IVAN—[*Half-asleep.*] Dot's gude. [*He tosses down his drink in one gulp.* OLSON *sips his ginger ale.* NICK *takes a swallow of his beer and then comes round the bar and goes out the door on left.*]

COCKY—[*Producing a sovereign.*] Ho there, you Fatty! Guv us another!

JOE—The saime, mates?

COCKY—Yus.

DRISCOLL—No, ye scut! I'll be havin' a pint av beer. I'm dhry as a loime kiln.

IVAN—[*Suddenly getting to his feet in a befuddled manner and nearly upsetting the table.*] I don' li-ike dis place! I wan' see girls—plenty girls. [*Pathetically.*] I don't li-ike dis place. I wan' dance with girl.

DRISCOLL—[*Pushing him back on his chair with a thud.*] Shut up, ye Rooshan baboon! A foine Romeo you'd make in your condishun. [IVAN *blubbers some incoherent protest—then suddenly falls asleep.*]

JOE—[*Bringing the drinks—looks at* OLSON.] An' you, matey?

OLSON—[*Shaking his head.*] Noting dis time, thank you.

COCKY—[*Mockingly.*] A-saivin' of 'is money, 'e is! Goin' back to 'ome an' mother. Goin' to buy a bloomin' farm an' punch the blarsted dirt, that's wot 'e is! [*Spitting disgustedly.*] There's a funny bird of a sailor man for yer, Gawd blimey!

OLSON—[*Wearing the same good-natured grin.*] Yust what I like, Cocky. I wus on farm long time when I wus kid.

DRISCOLL—Lave him alone, ye bloody insect! 'Tis a foine sight to see a man wid some sense in his head instead av a damn fool the loike av us. I only wisht I'd a mother alive to call me own. I'd not be dhrunk in this divil's hole this minute, maybe.

COCKY—[*Commencing to weep dolorously.*] Ow, down't talk, Drisc! I can't bear to 'ear you. I ain't never 'ad no mother, I ain't——

DRISCOLL—Shut up, ye ape, an' don't be makin' that squealin'. If ye cud see your ugly face, wid the big red nose av ye all screwed up in a knot, ye'd never shed a tear the rist av your loife. [*Roaring into song.*] We ar-re the byes av We-e-exford who fought wid hearrt an' hand! [*Speaking.*] To hell wid Ulster! [*He drinks and the others follow his example.*] An' I'll strip to any man in the city av London won't dhrink to that toast. [*He glares truculently at* JOE, *who immediately downs his beer.* NICK *enters again from the door on the left and comes up to* JOE *and whispers in his ear. The latter nods with satisfaction.*]

DRISCOLL—[*Glowering at them.*] What divil's thrick are ye up to now, the two av ye? [*He flourishes a brawny fist.*] Play fair wid us or ye deal wid me!

JOE—[*Hastily.*] No trick, shipmate! May Gawd kill me if that ain't troof!

NICK—[*Indicating* IVAN, *who is snoring.*] On'y your mate there was arskin' fur gels an' I thorght as 'ow yer'd like 'em to come dawn and 'ave a wet wiv yer.

JOE—[*With a smirking wink.*] Pretty, 'olesome gels they be, ain't they, Nick?"

NICK—Yus.

COCKY—Aar! I knows the gels you 'as, not 'arf! They'd fair blind yer, they're that 'omely. None of yer bloomin' gels fur me, ole Fatty. Me an' Drisc knows a place, down't we, Drisc?"

DRISCOLL—Divil a lie, we do. An' we'll be afther goin' there in a minute. There's music there an' a bit av a dance to liven a man.

JOE—Nick, 'ere, can play yer a tune, can't yer, Nick?

NICK—Yus.

JOE—An' yer can 'ave a dance in the side room 'ere.

DRISCOLL—Hurroo! Now you're talkin'. [*The two women,* FREDA *and* KATE, *enter from the left.*

FREDA *is a little, sallow-faced blonde.* KATE *is stout and dark.*]

COCKY—[*In a loud aside to* DRISCOLL.] Gawd blimey, look at 'em! Ain't they 'orrible? [*The women come forward to the table, wearing their best set smiles.*]

FREDA—[*In a raspy voice.*] 'Ullo, mates.

KATE—'Ad a good voyage?

DRISCOLL—Rotten; but no matther. Welcome, as the sayin' is, an' sit down, an' what'll ye be takin' for your thirst? [*To* KATE.] You'll be sittin' by me, darlin'—what's your name?

KATE—[*With a stupid grin.*] Kate. [*She stands by his chair.*]

DRISCOLL—[*Putting his arm around her.*] A good Irish name, but you're English by the trim av ye, an' be damned to you. But no matther. Ut's fat ye are, Katy dear, an' I never cud endure skinny wimin. [FREDA *favors him with a viperish glance and sits down by* OLSON.] What'll ye have?

OLSON—No, Drisc. Dis one bane on me. [*He takes out a roll of notes from his inside pocket and lays one on the table.* JOE, NICK, *and the women look at the money with greedy eyes.* IVAN *gives a particularly violent snore.*]

FREDA—Waike up your fren'. Gawd, 'ow I 'ates to 'ear snorin'.

DRISCOLL—[*Springing to action, smashes* IVAN'S *derby over his ears.*] D'you hear the lady talkin' to ye, ye Rooshan swab? [*The only reply to this is a snore.* DRISCOLL *pulls the battered remains of the derby off* IVAN's *head and smashes it back again.*] Arise an' shine, ye dhrunken swine! [*Another snore. The women giggle.* DRISCOLL *throws the beer left in his glass into* IVAN's *face. The Russian comes to in a flash, spluttering. There is a roar of laughter.*]

IVAN—[*Indignantly.*] I tell you—dot's someting I don' li-ike!

COCKY—Down't waste good beer, Drisc.

IVAN—[*Grumblingly.*] I tell you—dot is not ri-ight.

DRISCOLL—Ut's your own doin', Ivan. Ye was moanin' for girrls an' whin they come you sit gruntin' loike a pig in a sty. Have ye no manners? [IVAN *seems to see the women for the first time and grins foolishly.*]

KATE—[*Laughing at him.*] Cheero, ole chum, 'ows Russha?

IVAN—[*Greatly pleased—putting his hand in his pocket.*] I buy a drink.

OLSON—No; dis one bane on me. [*To* JOE.] Hey, you faller!"

JOE—Wot'll it be, Kate?"

KATE—Gin.

FREDA—Brandy.

DRISCOLL—An' Irish whiskey for the rist av us—

wid the excipshun av our timperance friend, God
pity him!

FREDA—[*To* OLSON.] You ain't drinkin'?

OLSON—[*Half-ashamed.*] No.

FREDA—[*With a seductive smile.*] I down't
blame yer. You got sense, you 'ave. I on'y tike
a nip o' brandy now an' agen fur my 'ealth. [JOE
brings the drinks and OLSON'S *change.* COCKY *gets
unsteadily to his feet and raises his glass in the air.*]

COCKY—'Ere's a toff toast for yer: The ladies,
Gawd— [*He hesitates—then adds in a grudging
tone.*]—bless 'em.

KATE—[*With a silly giggle.*] Oo-er! That
wasn't what you was goin' to say, you bad Cocky,
you! [*They all drink.*]

DRISCOLL—[*To* NICK.] Where's the tune ye was
promisin' to give us?

NICK—Come ahn in the side 'ere an' you'll 'ear it.

DRISCOLL—[*Getting up.*] Come on, all av ye.
We'll have a tune an' a dance if I'm not too dhrunk
to dance, God help me. [COCKY *and* IVAN *stagger
to their feet.* IVAN *can hardly stand. He is leer-
ing at* KATE *and snickering to himself in a maudlin
fashion. The three, led by* NICK, *go out the door on
the left.* KATE *follows them.* OLSON *and* FREDA
remain seated.]

COCKY—[*Calling over his shoulder.*] Come on
an' dance, Ollie.

OLSON—Yes, I come. [*He starts to get up.*

*From the side room comes the sound of an accordion
and a boisterous whoop from* DRISCOLL, *followed by
a heavy stamping of feet.*]

FREDA—Ow, down't go in there. Stay 'ere an'
'ave a talk wiv me. They're all drunk an' you ain't
drinkin'. [*With a smile up into his face.*] I'll
think yer don't like me if yer goes in there.

OLSON—[*Confused.*] You wus wrong, Miss
Freda. I don't—I mean I do like you.

FREDA—[*Smiling—puts her hand over his on the
table.*] An' I likes you. Yer a genelman. You
don't get drunk an' hinsult poor gels wot 'as a 'ard
an' uneppy life.

OLSON—[*Pleased but still more confused—wrig-
gling his feet.*] I bane drunk many time, Miss
Freda.

FREDA—Then why ain't yer drinkin' now? [*She
exchanges a quick, questioning glance with* JOE, *who
nods back at her—then she continues persuasively.*]
Tell me somethin' abaht yeself.

OLSON—[*With a grin.*] There ain't noting to
say, Miss Freda. I bane poor devil sailor man,
dat's all.

FREDA—Where was you born—Norway? [OLSON
shakes his head.] Denmark?

OLSON—No. You guess once more.

FREDA—Then it must be Sweden.

OLSON—Yes. I wus born in Stockholm.

FREDA—[*Pretending great delight.*] Ow, ain't

that funny! I was born there, too—in Stockholm.

OLSON—[*Astonished.*] You wus born in Sweden?

FREDA—Yes; you wouldn't think it, but it's Gawd's troof. [*She claps her hands delightedly.*]

OLSON—[*Beaming all over.*] You speak Swedish?

FREDA—[*Trying to smile sadly.*] Now. Y'see my ole man an' woman come 'ere to England when I was on'y a baby an' they was speakin' English b'fore I was old enough to learn. Sow I never knew Swedish. [*Sadly.*] Wisht I 'ad! [*With a smile.*] We'd 'ave a bloomin' lark of it if I 'ad, wouldn't we?

OLSON—It sound nice to hear the old talk yust once in a time.

FREDA—Righto! No place like yer 'ome, I says. Are yer goin' up to—to Stockholm b'fore yer ships away agen?

OLSON—Yes. I go home from here to Stockholm. [*Proudly.*] As passenger!

FREDA—An' you'll git another ship up there arter you've 'ad a vacation?

OLSON—No. I don't never ship on sea no more. I got all sea I want for my life—too much hard work for little money. Yust work, work, work on ship. I don't want more.

FREDA—Ow, I see. That's why you give up drinkin'.

OLSON—Yes. [*With a grin.*] If I drink I yust get drunk and spend all money.

FREDA—But if you ain't gointer be a sailor no more, what'll yer do? You been a sailor all yer life, ain't yer?

OLSON—No. I work on farm till I am eighteen. I like it, too—it's nice—work on farm.

FREDA—But ain't Stockholm a city same's London? Ain't no farms there, is there?

OLSON—We live—my brother and mother live— my father iss dead—on farm yust a little way from Stockholm. I have plenty money, now. I go back with two years' pay and buy more land yet; work on farm. [*Grinning.*] No more sea, no more bum grub, no more storms—yust nice work.

FREDA—Ow, ain't that luv'ly! I s'pose you'll be gittin' married, too?

OLSON—[*Very much confused.*] I don't know. I like to, if I find nice girl, maybe.

FREDA—Ain't yer got some gel back in Stockholm? I bet yer 'as.

OLSON—No. I got nice girl once before I go on sea. But I go on ship, and I don't come back, and she marry other faller. [*He grins sheepishly.*]

FREDA—Well, it's nice for yer to be goin' 'ome, anyway.

OLSON—Yes. I tank so. [*There is a crash from the room on left and the music abruptly stops. A moment later* COCKY *and* DRISCOLL *appear, support-*

ing the inert form of IVAN *between them.* **He is in the last stage of intoxication, unable to move a muscle.** NICK *follows them and sits down at the table in rear.*]

DRISCOLL—[*As they zigzag up to the bar.*] Ut's dead he is, I'm thinkin', for he's as limp as a blarsted corpse.

COCKY—[*Puffing.*] Gawd, 'e ain't 'arf 'eavy!

DRISCOLL—[*Slapping* IVAN's *face with his free hand.*] Wake up, ye divil, ye. Ut's no use. Gabriel's trumpet itself cudn't rouse him. [*To* JOE.] Give us a dhrink for I'm perishing wid the thirst. 'Tis harrd worrk, this.

JOE—Whiskey?

DRISCOLL—*Irish* whiskey, ye swab. [*He puts down a coin on the bar.* JOE *serves* COCKY *and* DRISCOLL. *They drink and then swerve over to* OLSON's *table.*]

OLSON—Sit down and rest for time, Drisc.

DRISCOLL—No, Ollie, we'll be takin' this lad home to his bed. Ut's late for wan so young to be out in the night. An' I'd not trust him in this hole as dhrunk as he is, an' him wid a full pay day on him. [*Shaking his fist at* JOE.] Oho, I know your games, me sonny bye!

JOE—[*With an air of grievance.*] There yer goes again—hinsultin' a 'onest man!

COCKY—Ho, listen to 'im! Guv 'im a shove in the marf, Drisc.

OLSON—[*Anxious to avoid a fight—getting up.*] I help you take Ivan to boarding house.

FREDA—[*Protestingly.*] Ow, you ain't gointer leave me, are yer? An' we 'avin' sech a nice talk, an' all.

DRISCOLL—[*With a wink.*] Ye hear what the lady says, Ollie. Ye'd best stay here, me timperance lady's man. An' we need no help. 'Tis only a bit av a way and we're two strong men if we are dhrunk. Ut's no hard shift to take the remains home. But ye can open the door for us, Ollie. [OLSON *goes to the door and opens it.*] Come on, Cocky, an' don't be fallin' aslape yourself. [*They lurch toward the door. As they go out* DRISCOLL *shouts back over his shoulder.*] We'll be comin' back in a short time, surely. So wait here for us, Ollie.

OLSON—All right. I wait here, Drisc. [*He stands in the doorway uncertainly.* JOE *makes violent signs to* FREDA *to bring him back. She goes over and puts her arm around* OLSON'S *shoulder.* JOE *motions to* NICK *to come to the bar. They whisper together excitedly.*]

FREDA—[*Coaxingly.*] You ain't gointer leave me, are yer, dearie? [*Then irritably.*] Fur Gawd's sake, shet that door! I'm fair freezin' to death wiv the fog. [OLSON *comes to himself with a start and shuts the door.*]

OLSON—[*Humbly.*] Excuse me, Miss Freda.

FREDA—[*Leading him back to the table—cough-*

ing.] Buy me a drink o' brandy, will yer? I'm sow cold.

OLSON—All you want, Miss Freda, all you want. [*To* JOE, *who is still whispering instructions to* NICK.] Hey, Yoe! Brandy for Miss Freda. [*He lays a coin on the table.*]

JOE—Righto! [*He pours out her drink and brings it to the table.*] 'Avin' somethink yeself, shipmate?

OLSON—No. I don't tank so. [*He points to his glass with a grin.*] Dis iss only belly-wash, no? [*He laughs.*]

JOE—[*Hopefully.*] 'Ave a man's drink.

OLSON—I would like to—but no. If I drink one I want drink cne tousand. [*He laughs again.*]

FREDA—[*Responding to a vicious nudge from* JOE'S *elbow.*] Ow, tike somethin'. I ain't gointer drink all be meself.

OLSON—Den give me a little yinger beer—small one. [JOE *goes back of the bar, making a sign to* NICK *to go to their table.* NICK *does so and stands so that the sailor cannot see what* JOE *is doing.*]

NICK—[*To make talk.*] Where's yer mates popped orf ter? [JOE *pours the contents of the little bottle into* OLSON'S *glass of ginger beer.*]—

OLSON—Dey take Ivan, dat drunk faller, to bed. They come back. [JOE *brings* OLSON'S *drink to the table and sets it before him.*]

JOE—[*To* NICK—*angrily.*] 'Op it, will yer? There ain't no time to be dawdlin'. See? 'Urry!

NICK—Down't worry, ole bird, I'm orf. [*He hurries out the door.* JOE *returns to his place behind the bar.*]

OLSON—[*After a pause—worriedly.*] I tank I should go after dem. Cocky iss very drunk, too, and Drisc——

FREDA—Aar! The big Irish is all right. Don't yer 'ear 'im say as 'ow they'd surely come back 'ere, an' fur you to wait fur 'em?

OLSON—Yes; but if dey don't come soon I tank I go see if dey are in boarding house all right.

FREDA—Where is the boardin' 'ouse?

OLSON—Yust little way back from street here.

FREDA—You stayin' there, too?

OLSON—Yes—until steamer sail for Stockholm— in two day.

FREDA—[*She is alternately looking at* JOE *and feverishly trying to keep* OLSON *talking so he will forget about going away after the others.*] Yer mother won't be arf glad to see yer agen, will she? [OLSON *smiles.*] Does she know yer comin'?

OLSON—No. I tought I would yust give her surprise. I write to her from Bonos Eres but I don't tell her I come home.

FREDA—Must be old, ain't she, yer ole lady?

OLSON—She iss eighty-two. [*He smiles reminiscently.*] You know, Miss Freda, I don't see my mother or my brother in—let me tank— [*He counts laboriously on his fingers.*] must be more than ten year. I write once in while and she write many time; and my brother he write me, too. My mother say in all letter I should come home right away. My brother he write same ting, too. He want me to help him on farm. I write back always I come soon; and I mean all time to go back home at end of voyage. But I come ashore, I take one drink, I take many drinks, I get drunk, I spend all money, I have to ship away for other voyage. So dis time I say to myself: Don't drink one drink, Ollie, or, sure, you don't get home. And I want go home dis time. I feel homesick for farm and to see my people again. [*He smiles.*] Yust like little boy, I feel homesick. Dat's why I don't drink noting to-night but dis—belly-wash! [*He roars with childish laughter, then suddenly becomes serious.*] You know, Miss Freda, my mother get very old, and I want see her. She might die and I would never——

FREDA—[*Moved a lot in spite of herself.*] Ow, don't talk like that! I jest 'ates to 'ear any one speakin' abaht dyin'. [*The door to the street is opened and* NICK *enters, followed by two rough-looking, shabbily-dressed men, wearing mufflers, with caps pulled down over their eyes. They sit at the table nearest to the door.* JOE *brings them three beers, and there is a whispered consultation, with many glances in the direction of* OLSON.]

OLSON—[*Starting to get up—worriedly.*] I tank I go round to boarding house. I tank someting go wrong with Drisc and Cocky.

FREDA—Ow, down't go. They kin take care of theyselves. They ain't babies. Wait 'arf a mo'. You ain't 'ad yer drink yet.

JOE—[*Coming hastily over to the table, indicates the men in the rear with a jerk of his thumb.*] One of them blokes wants yer to 'ave a wet wiv 'im.

FREDA—Righto! [*To* OLSON.] Let's drink this. [*She raises her glass. He does the same.*] 'Ere's a toast fur yer: Success to yer bloomin' farm an' may yer live long an' 'appy on it. Skoal! [*She tosses down her brandy. He swallows half his glass of ginger beer and makes a wry face.*]

OLSON—Skoal! [*He puts down his glass.*]

FREDA—[*With feigned indignation.*] Down't yer like my toast?

OLSON—[*Grinning.*] Yes. It iss very kind, Miss Freda.

FREDA—Then drink it all like I done.

OLSON—Well—— [*He gulps down the rest.*] Dere! [*He laughs.*]

FREDA—Done like a sport!

ONE OF THE ROUGHS—[*With a laugh.*] Amindra, ahoy!

NICK—[*Warningly.*] Sssshh!

OLSON—[*Turns around in his chair.*] Amindra?
Iss she in port? I sail on her once long time ago—
three mast, full rig, skys'l yarder? Iss dat ship
you mean?

THE ROUGH—[*Grinning.*] Yus; right you are.

OLSON—[*Angrily.*] I know dat damn ship—
worst ship dat sail to sea. Rotten grub and dey
make you work all time—and the Captain and Mate
wus Bluenose devils. No sailor who know anyting
ever ship on her. Where iss she bound from here?

THE ROUGH—Round Cape 'Orn—sails at daybreak.

OLSON—Py yingo, I pity poor fallers make dat
trip round Cape Stiff dis time year. I bet you
some of dem never see port once again. [*He passes
his hand over his eyes in a dazed way. His voice
grows weaker.*] Py golly, I feel dizzy. All the
room go round and round like I wus drunk. [*He
gets weakly to his feet.*] Good night, Miss Freda.
I bane feeling sick. Tell Drisc—I go home. [*He
takes a step forward and suddenly collapses over a
chair, rolls to the floor, and lies there unconscious.*]

JOE—[*From behind the bar.*] Quick, nawh!
[NICK *darts forward with* JOE *following.* FREDA *is
already beside the unconscious man and has taken
the roll of money from his inside pocket. She strips
off a note furtively and shoves it into her bosom,
trying to conceal her action, but* JOE *sees her.
She hands the roll to* JOE, *who pockets it.* NICK

goes through all the other pockets and lays a handful of change on the table.]

JOE—[*Impatiently.*] 'Urry, 'urry, can't yer? The other blokes'll be 'ere in 'arf a mo'. [*The two roughs come forward.*] 'Ere, you two, tike 'im in under the arms like 'e was drunk. [*They do so.*] Tike 'im to the Amindra—yer knows that, don't yer?—two docks above. Nick'll show yer. An' you, Nick, down't yer leave the bleedin' ship till the capt'n guvs yer this bloke's advance—full month's pay—five quid, d'yer 'ear?

NICK—I knows me bizness, ole bird. [*They support* OLSON *to the door.*]

THE ROUGH—[*As they are going out.*] This silly bloke'll 'ave the s'prise of 'is life when 'e wakes up on board of 'er. [*They laugh. The door closes behind them.* FREDA *moves quickly for the door on the left but* JOE *gets in her way and stops her.*]

JOE—[*Threateningly.*] Guv us what yer took!

FREDA—Took? I guv yer all 'e 'ad.

JOE—Yer a liar! I seen yer a-playin' yer sneakin' tricks, but yer can't fool Joe. I'm too old a 'and. [*Furiously.*] Guv it to me, yer bloody cow! [*He grabs her by the arm.*]

FREDA—Lemme alone! I ain't got no——

JOE—[*Hits her viciously on the side of the jaw. She crumples up on the floor.*] That'll learn yer! [*He stoops down and fumbles in her bosom and pulls out the banknote, which he stuffs into his pocket with a grunt of satisfaction.* KATE *opens the door on the left and looks in—then rushes to* FREDA *and lifts her head up in her arms.*]

KATE—[*Gently.*] Pore dearie! [*Looking at* JOE *angrily.*] Been 'ittin' 'er agen, 'ave yer, yer cowardly swine!

JOE—Yus; an' I'll 'it you, too, if yer don't keep yer marf shut. Tike 'er aht of 'ere! [KATE *carries* FREDA *into the next room.* JOE *goes behind the bar. A moment later the outer door is opened and* DRISCOLL *and* COCKY *come in.*]

DRISCOLL—Come on, Ollie. [*He suddenly sees that* OLSON *is not there, and turns to* JOE.] Where is ut he's gone to?

JOE—[*With a meaning wink.*] 'E an' Freda went aht t'gether 'bout five minutes past. 'E's fair gone on 'er, 'e is.

DRISCOLL—[*With a grin.*] Oho, so that's ut, is ut? Who'd think Ollie'd be sich a divil wid the wimin? 'Tis lucky he's sober or she'd have him stripped to his last ha'penny. [*Turning to* COCKY, *who is blinking sleepily.*] What'll ye have, ye little scut? [*To* JOE.] Give me whiskey, *Irish* whiskey!

[*The Curtain Falls*]

IN THE ZONE

A Play In One Act

CHARACTERS

Smitty
Davis
Swanson
Scotty
Ivan
Paul
Jack
Driscoll
Cocky

Seamen on the British Tramp Steamer Glencairn

IN THE ZONE

SCENE—*The seamen's forecastle. On the right above the bunks three or four portholes covered with black cloth can be seen. On the floor near the doorway is a pail with a tin dipper. A lantern in the middle of the floor, turned down very low, throws a dim light around the place. Five men,* SCOTTY, IVAN, SWANSON, SMITTY *and* PAUL, *are in their bunks apparently asleep. It is about ten minutes of twelve on a night in the fall of the year 1915.*

SMITTY *turns slowly in his bunk and, leaning out over the side, looks from one to another of the men as if to assure himself that they are asleep. Then he climbs carefully out of his bunk and stands in the middle of the forecastle fully dressed, but in his stocking feet, glancing around him suspiciously. Reassured, he leans down and cautiously pulls out a suit-case from under the bunks in front of him.*

Just at this moment DAVIS *appears in the doorway, carrying a large steaming coffee-pot in his hand. He stops short when he sees*

85

SMITTY. *A puzzled expression comes over his face, followed by one of suspicion, and he retreats farther back in the alleyway, where he can watch* SMITTY *without being seen.*

All the latter's movements indicate a fear of discovery. He takes out a small bunch of keys and unlocks the suit-case, making a slight noise as he does so. SCOTTY *wakes up and peers at him over the side of the bunk.* SMITTY *opens the suit-case and takes out a small black tin box, carefully places this under his mattress, shoves the suit-case back under the bunk, climbs into his bunk again, closes his eyes and begins to snore loudly.*

DAVIS *enters the forecastle, places the coffee-pot beside the lantern, and goes from one to the other of the sleepers and shakes them vigorously, saying to each in a low voice:* Near eight bells, Scotty. Arise and shine, Swanson. Eight bells, Ivan. SMITTY *yawns loudly with a great pretense of having been dead asleep. All of the rest of the men tumble out of their bunks, stretching and gaping, and commence to pull on their shoes. They go one by one to the cupboard near the open door, take out their cups and spoons, and sit down together on the benches. The coffee-pot is passed around. They munch their biscuits and sip their coffee in dull silence.*

DAVIS—[*Suddenly jumping to his feet—nervously.*] Where's that air comin' from? [*All are startled and look at him wonderingly.*]

SWANSON—[*A squat, surly-faced Swede—grumpily.*] What air? I don't feel nothing.

DAVIS—[*Excitedly.*] I kin feel it—a draft. [*He stands on the bench and looks around—suddenly exploding.*] Damn fool square-head! [*He leans over the upper bunk in which* PAUL *is sleeping and slams the porthole shut.*] I got a good notion to report him. Serve him bloody well right! What's the use o' blindin' the ports when that thick-head goes an' leaves 'em open?

SWANSON—[*Yawning—too sleepy to be aroused by anything—carelessly.*] Dey don't see what little light go out yust one port.

SCOTTY—[*Protestingly.*] Dinna be a loon, Swanson! D'ye no ken the dangerr o' showin' a licht wi' a pack o' submarrines lyin' aboot?

IVAN—[*Shaking his shaggy ox-like head in an emphatic affirmative.*] Dot's right, Scotty. I don' li-ike blow up, no, by devil!

SMITTY—[*His manner slightly contemptuous.*] I don't think there's much danger of meeting any of their submarines, not until we get into the War Zone, at any rate.

DAVIS—[*He and* SCOTTY *look at* SMITTY *suspiciously—harshly.*] You don't, eh? [*He lowers his voice and speaks slowly.*] Well, we're in the war zone right this minit if you wants to know. [*The effect of this speech is instantaneous. All sit bolt upright on their benches and stare at Davis.*]

SMITTY—How do you know, Davis?

DAVIS—[*Angrily.*] 'Cos Drisc heard the First send the Third below to wake the skipper when we fetched the zone—bout five bells, it was. Now whata y' got to say?

SMITTY—[*Conciliatingly.*] Oh, I wasn't doubting your word, Davis; but you know they're not pasting up bulletins to let the crew know when the zone is reached—especially on ammunition ships like this.

IVAN—[*Decidedly.*] I don't li-ike dees voyage. Next time I ship on windjammer Boston to River Plate, load with wood only so it float, by golly!

SWANSON—[*Fretfully.*] I hope British navy blow 'em to hell, those submarines, py damn!

SCOTTY—[*Looking at* SMITTY, *who is staring at the doorway in a dream, his chin on his hands. Meaningly.*] It is no the submarrines only we've to fear, I'm thinkin'.

DAVIS—[*Assenting eagerly.*] That's no lie, Scotty.

SWANSON—You mean the mines?

SCOTTY—I wasna thinkin' o' mines eitherr.

DAVIS—There's many a good ship blown up and at the bottom of the sea, what never hit no mine or torpedo.

Scotty—Did ye neverr read of the Gerrman spies and the dirrty work they're doin' all the war? [*He and* Davis *both glance at* Smitty, *who is deep in thought and is not listening to the conversation.*]

Davis—An' the clever way they fool you!

Swanson—Sure; I read it in paper many time.

Davis—Well—[*He is about to speak but hesitates and finishes lamely*] you got to watch out, that's all I says.

Ivan—[*Drinking the last of his coffee and slamming his fist on the bench explosively.*] I tell you dis rotten coffee give me belly-ache, yes! [*They all look at him in amused disgust.*]

Scotty—[*Sardonically.*] Dinna fret about it, Ivan. If we blow up ye'll no be mindin' the pain in your middle. [Jack *enters. He is a young American with a tough, good-natured face. He wears dungarees and a heavy jersey.*]

Jack—Eight bells, fellers.

Ivan—[*Stupidly.*] I don' hear bell ring.

Jack—No, and yuh won't hear any ring, yuh boob—[*Lowering his voice unconsciously.*] now we're in the war zone.

Swanson—[*Anxiously.*] Is the boats all ready?

Jack—Sure; we can lower 'em in a second.

Davis—A lot o' good the boats'll do, with us loaded deep with all kinds o' dynamite and stuff the like o' that! If a torpedo hits this hooker we'll all be in hell b'fore you could wink your eye.

JACK—They ain't goin' to hit us, see? That's my dope. Whose wheel is it?

IVAN—[*Sullenly.*] My wheel. [*He lumbers out.*]

JACK—And whose lookout?

SWANSON—Mine, I tink. [*He follows* IVAN.]

JACK—[*Scornfully.*] A hell of a lot of use keepin' a lookout! We couldn't run away or fight if we wanted to. [*To* SCOTTY *and* SMITTY.] Better look up the bo'sun or the Fourth, you two, and let 'em see you're awake. [SCOTTY *goes to the doorway and turns to wait for* SMITTY, *who is still in the same position, head on hands, seemingly unconscious of everything.* JACK *slaps him roughly on the shoulder and he comes to with a start.*] Aft and report, Duke! What's the matter with yuh—in a dope dream? [SMITTY *goes out after* SCOTTY *without answering.* JACK *looks after him with a frown.*] He's a queer guy. I can't figger him out.

DAVIS—Nor no one else. [*Lowering his voice—meaningly.*] An' he's liable to turn out queerer than any of us think if we ain't careful.

JACK—[*Suspiciously.*] What d'yuh mean? [*They are interrupted by the entrance of* DRISCOLL *and* COCKY.]

COCKY—[*Protestingly.*] Blimey if I don't fink I'll put in this 'ere watch ahtside on deck. [*He and* DRISCOLL *go over and get their cups.*] I down't want to be caught in this 'ole if they 'its us. [*He pours out coffee.*]

DRISCOLL—[*Pouring his.*] Divil a bit ut wud matther where ye arre. Ye'd be blown to smithereens
b'fore ye cud say your name. [*He sits down, over-
turning as he does so the untouched cup of coffee
which* SMITTY *had forgotten and left on the bench.
They all jump nervously as the tin cup hits the
floor with a bang.* DRISCOLL *flies into an unreason-
ing rage.*] Who's the dirty scut left this cup where
a man 'ud sit on ut?

DAVIS—It's Smitty's.

DRISCOLL—[*Kicking the cup across the forecastle.*] Does he think he's too much av a bloody
gentleman to put his own away loike the rist av us?
If he does I'm the bye'll beat that noshun out av
his head.

COCKY—Be the airs 'e puts on you'd think 'e was
the Prince of Wales. Wot's 'e doin' on a ship,
I arsks yer? 'E ain't now good as a sailor, is 'e?—
dawdlin' abaht on deck like a chicken wiv 'is 'ead
cut orf!

JACK—[*Good-naturedly.*] Aw, the Duke's all
right. S'posin' he did ferget his cup—what's the
dif? [*He picks up the cup and puts it away—
with a grin.*] This war zone stuff's got yer goat,
Drisc—and yours too, Cocky—and I ain't cheerin'
much fur it myself, neither.

COCKY—[*With a sigh.*] Blimey, it ain't no
bleedin' joke, yer first trip, to know as there's a
ship full of shells li'ble to go orf in under your

bloomin' feet, as you might say, if we gets 'it be a torpedo or mine. [*With sudden savagery.*] Calls theyselves 'uman bein's, too! Blarsted 'Uns!

DRISCOLL—[*Gloomily.*] 'Tis me last trip in the bloody zone, God help me. The divil take their twenty-foive percent bonus—and be drowned like a rat in a trap in the bargain, maybe.

DAVIS—Wouldn't be so bad if she wasn't carryin' ammunition. Them's the kind the subs is layin' for.

DRISCOLL—[*Irritably.*] Fur the love av hivin, don't be talkin' about ut. I'm sick wid thinkin' and jumpin' at iviry bit av a noise. [*There is a pause during which they all stare gloomily at the floor.*]

JACK—Hey, Davis, what was you sayin' about Smitty when they come in?

DAVIS—[*With a great air of mystery.*] I'll tell you in a minit. I want to wait an' see if he's comin' back. [*Impressively.*] You won't be callin' him all right when you hears what I seen with my own eyes. [*He adds with an air of satisfaction.*] An' you won't be feelin' no safer, neither. [*They all look at him with puzzled glances full of a vague apprehension.*]

DRISCOLL—God blarst ut! [*He fills his pipe and lights it. The others, with an air of remembering something they had forgotten, do the same. SCOTTY enters.*]

SCOTTY—[*In awed tones.*] Mon, but it's clear outside the nicht! Like day.

DAVIS—[*In low tones.*] Where's Smitty, Scotty?

SCOTTY—Out on the hatch starin' at the moon like a mon half-daft.

DAVIS—Kin you see him from the doorway?

SCOTTY—[*Goes to doorway and carefully peeks out.*] Aye; he's still there.

DAVIS—Keep your eyes on him for a moment. I've got something I wants to tell the boys and I don't want him walkin' in in the middle of it. Give a shout if he starts this way.

SCOTTY—[*With suppressed excitement.*] Aye, I'll watch him. And I've somethin' myself to tell aboot his Lordship.

DRISCOLL—[*Impatiently.*] Out wid ut! You're talkin' more than a pair av auld women wud be standin' in the road, and gittin' no further along.

DAVIS—Listen! You 'member when I went to git the coffee, Jack?

JACK—Sure, I do.

DAVIS—Well, I brings it down here same as usual and got as far as the door there when I sees him.

JACK—Smitty?

DAVIS—Yes, Smitty! He was standin' in the middle of the fo'c's'tle there [*Pointing.*] lookin' around sneakin'-like at Ivan and Swanson and the rest 's if he wants to make certain they're asleep. [*He pauses significantly, looking from one to the other of his listeners.* Scotty *is nervously dividing his attention between* Smitty *on the hatch outside and* Davis' *story, fairly bursting to break in with his own revelations.*]

Jack—[*Impatiently.*] What of it?

Davis—Listen! He was standin' right there— [*Pointing again.*] in his stockin' feet—no shoes on, mind, so he wouldn't make no noise!

Jack—[*Spitting disgustedly.*] Aw!

Davis—[*Not heeding the interruption.*] I seen right away somethin' on the queer was up so I slides back into the alleyway where I kin see him but he can't see me. After he makes sure they're all asleep he goes in under the bunks there—bein' careful not to raise a noise, mind!—an' takes out his bag there. [*By this time every one,* Jack *included, is listening breathlessly to his story.*) Then he fishes in his pocket an' takes out a bunch o' keys an' kneels down beside the bag an' opens it.

Scotty—[*Unable to keep silent longer.*] Mon, didn't I see him do that same thing wi' these two eyes. 'Twas just that moment I woke and spied him.

Davis—[*Surprised, and a bit nettled to have to share his story with any one.*] Oh, you seen him, too, eh? [*To the others.*] Then Scotty kin tell you if I'm lyin' or not.

Driscoll—An' what did he do whin he'd the bag opened?

Davis—He bends down and reaches out his hand sort o' scared-like, like it was somethin' dang'rous he was after, an' feels round in under his duds— hidden in under his duds an' wrapped up in 'em, it was—an' he brings out a black iron box!

Cocky—[*Looking around him with a frightened glance.*] Gawd blimey! [*The others likewise betray their uneasiness, shuffling their feet nervously.*]

Davis—Ain't that right, Scotty?

Scotty—Right as rain, I'm tellin' ye'!

Davis—[*To the others with an air of satisfaction.*] There you are! [*Lowering his voice.*] An' then what d'you suppose he did? Sneaks to his bunk an' slips the black box in under his mattress— in under his mattress, mind!—

Jack—And it's there now?

Davis—Course it is! [*Jack starts toward Smitty's bunk. Driscoll grabs him by the arm.*]

Driscoll—Don't be touchin' ut, Jack!

Jack—Yuh needn't worry. I ain't goin' to touch it. [*He pulls up Smitty's mattress and looks down. The others stare at him, holding their breaths. He turns to them, trying hard to assume a careless tone.*] It's there, aw right.

Cocky—[*Miserably upset.*] I'm gointer 'op it aht on deck. [*He gets up but Driscoll pulls him down agcin. Cocky protests.*] It fair guvs me the trembles sittin' still in 'ere.

Driscoll—[*Scornfully.*] Are ye frightened, ye

toad? 'Tis a hell av a thing fur grown men to be shiverin' loike childer at a bit av a black box. [*Scratching his head in uneasy perplexity.*] Still, ut's damn queer, the looks av ut.

DAVIS—[*Sarcastically.*] A bit of a black box, eh? How big d'you think them—[*He hesitates*]— things has to be—big as this fo'c's'tle?

JACK—[*In a voice meant to be reassuring.*] Aw, hell! I'll bet it ain't nothin' but some coin he's saved he's got locked up in there.

DAVIS—[*Scornfully.*] That's likely, ain't it? Then why does he act so s'picious? He's been on ship near two year, ain't he? He knows damn well there ain't no thiefs in this fo'c's'tle, don't he? An' you know 's well 's I do he didn't have no money when he came on board an' he ain't saved none since. Don't you? [*JACK doesn't answer.*] Listen! D'you know what he done after he put that thing in under his mattress?—an' Scotty'll tell you if I ain't speakin' truth. He looks round to see if any one's woke up——

SCOTTY—I clapped my eyes shut when he turned round.

DAVIS—An' then he crawls into his bunk an' shuts his eyes, an' starts in *snorin'*, *pretendin'* he was asleep, mind!

SCOTTY—Aye, I could hear him.

DAVIS—An' when I goes to call him I don't even shake him. I just says, "Eight bells, Smitty," in a'most a whisper-like, an' up he gets yawnin' an' stretchin' fit to kill hisself 's if he'd been dead asleep.

COCKY—Gawd blimey!

DRISCOLL—[*Shaking his head.*] Ut looks bad, divil a doubt av ut.

DAVIS—[*Excitedly.*] An' now I come to think of it, there's the porthole. How'd it come to git open, tell me that? I know'd well Paul never opened it. Ain't he grumblin' about bein' cold all the time?

SCOTTY—The mon that opened it meant no good to this ship, whoever he was.

JACK—[*Sourly.*] What porthole? What're yuh talkin' about?

DAVIS—[*Pointing over* PAUL's *bunk.*] There. It was open when I come in. I felt the cold air on my neck an' shut it. It would'a been clear's a lighthouse to any sub that was watchin'—an' we s'posed to have all the ports blinded! Who'd do a dirty trick like that? It wasn't none of us, nor Scotty here, nor Swanson, nor Ivan. Who would it be, then?

COCKY—[*Angrily.*] Must'a been 'is bloody Lordship.

DAVIS—For all's we know he might'a been signallin' with it. They does it like that by winkin' a light. Ain't you read how they gets caught doin' it in London an' on the coast?

COCKY—[*Firmly convinced now.*] An' wots 'e

doin' aht alone on the 'atch—keepin' 'isself clear of us like 'e was afraid?

DRISCOLL—Kape your eye on him, Scotty.

SCOTTY—There's no a move oot o' him.

JACK—[*In irritated perplexity.*] But, hell, ain't he an Englishman? What'd he wanta——

DAVIS—English? How d'we know he's English? Cos he talks it? That ain't no proof. Ain't you read in the papers how all them German spies they been catchin' in England has been livin' there for ten, often as not twenty years, an' talks English as good's any one? An' look here, ain't you noticed he don't talk natural? He talks it too damn good, that's what I mean. He don't talk exactly like a toff, does he, Cocky?

COCKY—Not like any toff as I ever met up wiv.

DAVIS—No; an' he don't talk it like us, that's certain. An' he don't look English. An' what d'we know about him when you come to look at it? Nothin'! He ain't ever said where he comes from or why. All we knows is he ships on here in London 'bout a year b'fore the war starts, as an A. B.— stole his papers most lik'ly—when he don't know how to box the compass, hardly. Ain't that queer in itself? An' was he ever open with us like a good shipmate? No; he's always had that sly air about him 's if he was hidin' somethin'.

DRISCOLL—[*Slapping his thigh—angrily.*] Divil

take me if I don't think ye have the truth av ut, Davis.

Cocky—[*Scornfully.*] Lettin' on be 'is silly airs, and all, 'e's the son of a blarsted earl or somethink!

Davis—An' the name he calls hisself—Smith! I'd risk a quid of my next pay day that his real name is Schmidt, if the truth was known.

Jack—[*Evidently fighting against his own conviction.*] Aw, say, you guys give me a pain! What'd they want puttin' a spy on this old tub for?

Davis—[*Shaking his head sagely.*] They're deep ones, an' there's a lot o' things a sailor'll see in the ports he puts in ought to be useful to 'em. An' if he kin signal to 'em an' they blows us up it's one ship less, ain't it? [*Lowering his voice and indicating* Smitty's *bunk.*] Or if he blows us up hisself.

Scotty—[*In alarmed tones.*] Hush, mon! Here he comes! [Scotty *hurries over to a bench and sits down. A thick silence settles over the forecastle. The men look from one to another with uneasy glances.* Smitty *enters and sits down beside his bunk. He is seemingly unaware of the dark glances of suspicion directed at him from all sides. He slides his hand back stealthily over his mattress and his fingers move, evidently feeling to make sure the box is still there. The others follow this movement carefully with quick looks out of the corners of their eyes. Their attitudes grow tense as if they were about to spring at him. Satisfied the box is safe,* SMITTY *draws his hand away slowly and utters a sigh of relief.*]

SMITTY—[*In a casual tone which to them sounds sinister.*] It's a good light night for the subs if there's any about. [*For a moment he sits staring in front of him. Finally he seems to sense the hostile atmosphere of the forecastle and looks from one to the other of the men in surprise. All of them avoid his eyes. He sighs with a puzzled expression and gets up and walks out of the doorway. There is silence for a moment after his departure and then a storm of excited talk breaks loose.*]

DAVIS—Did you see him feelin' if it was there?

COCKY—'E ain't arf a sly one wiv 'is talk of submarines, Gawd blind 'im!

SCOTTY—Did ye see the sneakin' looks he gave us?

DRISCOLL—If ivir I saw black shame on a man's face 'twas on his whin he sat there!

JACK—[*Thoroughly convinced at last.*] He looked bad to me. He's a crook, aw right.

DAVIS—[*Excitedly.*] What'll we do? We gotter do somethin' quick or—— [*He is interrupted by the sound of something hitting against the port side of the forecastle with a dull, heavy thud. The men start to their feet in wild-eyed terror and turn as if they were going to rush for the deck. They stand that way for a strained moment, scarcely breathing and listening intently.*]

JACK—[*With a sickly smile.*] Hell! It's on'y a piece of driftwood or a floatin' log. [*He sits down again.*]

DAVIS—[*Sarcastically.*] Or a mine that didn't go off—that time—or a piece o' wreckage from some ship they've sent to Davy Jones.

COCKY—[*Mopping his brow with a trembling hand.*] Blimey! [*He sinks back weakly on a bench.*]

DRISCOLL—[*Furiously.*] God blarst ut! No man at all cud be puttin' up wid the loike av this— an' I'm not wan to be fearin' anything or any man in the worrld'll stand up to me face to face; but this divil's trickery in the darrk—— [*He starts for SMITTY's bunk.*] I'll throw ut out wan av the portholes an' be done wid ut. [*He reaches toward the mattress.*]

SCOTTY—[*Grabbing his arm—wildly.*] Arre ye daft, mon?

DAVIS—Don't monkey with it, Drisc. I knows what to do. Bring the bucket o' water here, Jack, will you? [*JACK gets it and brings it over to DAVIS.*] An' you, Scotty, see if he's back on the hatch.

SCOTTY—[*Cautiously peering out.*] Aye, he's sittin' there the noo.

DAVIS—Sing out if he makes a move. Lift up

the mattress, Drisc—careful now! [DRISCOLL *does so with infinite caution.*] Take it out, JACK— careful—don't shake it now, for Christ's sake! Here—put it in the water—easy! There, that's fixed it! [*They all sit down with great sighs of relief.*] The water'll git in and spoil it.

DRISCOLL—[*Slapping* DAVIS *on the back.*] Good wurrk for ye, Davis, ye scut! [*He spits on his hands aggressively.*] An' now what's to be done wid that black-hearted thraitor?

COCKY—[*Belligerently.*] Guv 'im a shove in the marf and 'eave 'im over the side!

DAVIS—An' serve him right!

JACK—Aw, say, give him a chance. Yuh can't prove nothin' till yuh find out what's in there.

DRISCOLL—[*Heatedly.*] Is ut more proof ye'd be needin' afther what we've seen an' heard? Then listen to me—an' ut's Driscoll talkin'—if there's divilmint in that box an' we see plain 'twas his plan to murrdher his own shipmates that have served him fair—— [*He raises his fist.*] I'll choke his rotten hearrt out wid me own hands, an' over the side wid him, and one man missin' in the mornin'.

DAVIS—An' no one the wiser. He's the balmy kind what commits suicide.

COCKY—They 'angs spies ashore.

JACK—[*Resentfully.*] If he's done what yuh think I'll croak him myself. Is that good enough for yuh?

DRISCOLL—[*Looking down at the box.*] How'll we be openin' this, I wonder?

SCOTTY—[*From the doorway—warningly.*] He's standin' up.

DAVIS—We'll take his keys away from him when he comes in. Quick, Drisc! You an' Jack get beside the door and grab him. [*They get on either side of the door.* DAVIS *snatches a small coil of rope from one of the upper bunks.*] This'll do for me an' Scotty to tie him.

SCOTTY—He's turrnin' this way—he's comin'! [*He moves away from door.*]

DAVIS—Stand by to lend a hand, Cocky.

COCKY—Righto. [*As* SMITTY *enters the forecastle he is seized roughly from both sides and his arms pinned behind him. At first he struggles fiercely, but seeing the uselessness of this, he finally stands calmly and allows* DAVIS *and* SCOTTY *to tie up his arms.*]

SMITTY—[*When they have finished—with cold contempt.*] If this is your idea of a joke I'll have to confess it's a bit too thick for me to enjoy.

COCKY—[*Angrily.*] Shut yer marf, 'ear!

DRISCOLL—[*Roughly.*] Ye'll find ut's no joke, me bucko, b'fore we're done wid you. [*To* SCOTTY.] Kape your eye peeled, Scotty, and sing out if any one's comin'. [SCOTTY *resumes his post at the door.*]

SMITTY—[*With the same icy contempt.*] If you'd be good enough to explain——

DRISCOLL—[*Furiously.*] Explain, is ut? 'Tis you'll do the explainin'—an' damn quick, or we'll know the reason why. [*To* JACK *and* DAVIS.] Bring him here, now. [*They push* SMITTY *over to the bucket.*] Look here, ye murrderin' swab. D'you see ut? [SMITTY *looks down with an expression of amazement which rapidly changes to one of anguish.*]

DAVIS—[*With a sneer.*] Look at him! S'prised, ain't you? If you wants to try your dirty spyin' tricks on us you've gotter git up earlier in the mornin'.

COCKY—Thorght yer weren't 'arf a fox, didn't yer?

SMITTY—[*Trying to restrain his growing rage.*] What—what do you mean? That's only—How dare—What are you doing with my private belongings?

COCKY—[*Sarcastically.*] Ho yus! Private b'longings!

DRISCOLL—[*Shouting.*] What is ut, ye swine? Will you tell us to our faces? What's in ut?

SMITTY—[*Biting his lips—holding himself in check with a great effort.*] Nothing but—— That's my business. You'll please attend to your own.

DRISCOLL—Oho, ut is, is ut? [Shaking his fist *in* SMITTY'S *face.*] Talk aisy now if ye know

what's best for you. Your business, indade! Then
we'll be makin' ut ours, I'm thinkin'. [*To* JACK
and DAVIS.] Take his keys away from him an'
we'll see if there's one'll open ut, maybe. [*They
start in searching* SMITTY, *who tries to resist and
kicks out at the bucket.* DRISCOLL *leaps forward
and helps them push him away.*] Try to kick ut
over, wud ye? Did ye see him then? Tryin' to
murrdher us all, the scut! Take that pail out av
his way, Cocky. [SMITTY *struggles with all of his
strength and keeps them busy for a few seconds.
As* COCKY *grabs the pail* SMITTY *makes a final effort
and, lunging forward, kicks again at the bucket but
only succeeds in hitting* COCKY *on the shin.* COCKY
*immediately sets down the pail with a bang and,
clutching his knee in both hands, starts hopping
around the forecastle, groaning and swearing.*]

COCKY—Ooow! Gawd strike me pink! Kicked
me, 'e did! Bloody, bleedin', rotten Dutch 'og!
[*Approaching* SMITTY, *who has given up the fight
and is pushed back against the wall near the doorway with* JACK *and* DAVIS *holding him on either
side—wrathfully, at the top of his lungs.*] Kick
me, will yer? I'll show yer what for, yer bleedin'
sneak! [*He draws back his fist.* DRISCOLL *pushes
him to one side.*]

DRISCOLL—Shut your mouth! D'you want to
wake the whole ship? [COCKY *grumbles and retires
to a bench, nursing his sore shin.*]

JACK—[*Taking a small bunch of keys from* SMITTY'*s pocket.*] Here yuh are, Drisc.

DRISCOLL—[*Taking them.*] We'll soon be knowin'. [*He takes the pail and sits down, placing it on the floor between his feet.* SMITTY *again tries to break loose but he is too tired and is easily held back against the wall.*]

SMITTY—[*Breathing heavily and very pale.*] Cowards!

JACK—[*With a growl.*] Nix on the rough talk, see! That don't git yuh nothin'.

DRISCOLL—[*Looking at the lock on the box in the water and then scrutinizing the keys in his hand.*] This'll be ut, I'm thinkin'. [*He selects one and gingerly reaches his hand in the water.*]

SMITTY—[*His face grown livid—chokingly.*] Don't you open that box, Driscoll. If you do, so help me God, I'll kill you if I have to hang for it.

DRISCOLL—[*Pausing—his hand in the water.*] Whin I open this box I'll not be the wan to be kilt, me sonny bye! I'm no dirty spy.

SMITTY—[*His voice trembling with rage. His eyes are fixed on* DRISCOLL'*s hand.*] Spy? What are you talking about? I only put that box there so I could get it quick in case we were torpedoed. Are you all mad? Do you think I'm—— [*Chokingly.*] You stupid curs! You cowardly dolts! [DAVIS *claps his hand over* SMITTY'*s mouth.*]

DAVIS—That'll be enough from you! [DRISCOLL

*takes the dripping box from the water and starts
to fit in the key.* SMITTY *springs forward furiously, almost escaping from their grasp, and drags
them after him half-way across the forecastle.*]

DRISCOLL—Hold him, ye divils! [*He puts the
box back in the water and jumps to their aid.*
COCKY *hovers on the outskirts of the battle, mindful of the kick he received.*]

SMITTY—[*Raging.*] Cowards! Damn you! Rotten curs! [*He is thrown to the floor and held
there.*] Cowards! Cowards!

DRISCOLL—I'll shut your dirty mouth for you.
[*He goes to his bunk and pulls out a big wad of
waste and comes back to* SMITTY.]

SMITTY—Cowards! Cowards!

DRISCOLL—[*With no gentle hand slaps the waste
over* SMITTY'S *mouth.*] That'll teach you to be
misnamin' a man, ye sneak. Have ye a handkerchief, Jack? [JACK *hands him one and he ties it
tightly around* SMITTY'S *head over the waste.*]
That'll fix your gab. Stand him up, now, and tie
his feet, too, so he'll not be movin'. [*They do so
and leave him with his back against the wall near*
SCOTTY. *Then they all sit down beside* DRISCOLL,
*who again lifts the box out of the water and sets
it carefully on his knees. He picks out the key,
then hesitates, looking from one to the other uncertainly.*] We'd best be takin' this to the skipper,
d'you think, maybe?

JACK—[*Irritably.*]   To hell with the Old Man. This is our game and we c'n play it without no help.

COCKY—Now bleedin' horficers, I says!

DAVIS—They'd only be takin' all the credit and makin' heroes of theyselves.

DRISCOLL—[*Boldly.*]   Here goes, thin!   [*He slowly turns the key in the lock. The others instinctively turn away. He carefully pushes the cover back on its hinges and looks at what he sees inside with an expression of puzzled astonishment. The others crowd up close.   Even* SCOTTY *leaves his post to take a look.*]   What is ut, Davis?

DAVIS—[*Mystified.*]   Looks funny, don't it? Somethin' square tied up in a rubber bag.   Maybe it's dynamite—or somethin'—you can't never tell.

JACK—Aw, it ain't got no works so it ain't no bomb, I'll bet.

DAVIS—[*Dubiously.*]   They makes them all kinds, they do.

JACK—Open it up, Drisc.

DAVIS—Careful now!   [DRISCOLL *takes a black rubber bag resembling a large tobacco pouch from the box and unties the string which is wound tightly around the top.   He opens it and takes out a small packet of letters also tied up with string.   He turns these over in his hands and looks at the others questioningly.*]

JACK—[*With a broad grin.*]   On'y letters!

[*Slapping* DAVIS *on the back.*] Yuh're a hell of a Sherlock Holmes, ain't yuh? Letters from his best girl too, I'll bet. Let's turn the Duke loose, what d'yuh say? [*He starts to get up.*]

DAVIS—[*Fixing him with a withering look.*] Don't be so damn smart, Jack. Letters, you says, 's if there never was no harm in 'em. How d'you s'pose spies gets their orders and sends back what they finds out if it ain't by letters and such things? There's many a letter is worser'n any bomb.

COCKY—Righto! They ain't as innercent as they looks, I'll take me oath, when you read 'em. [*Pointing at* SMITTY.] Not 'is Lordship's letters; not be no means!

JACK—[*Sitting down again.*] Well, read 'em and find out. [DRISCOLL *commences untying the packet. There is a muffled groan of rage and protest from* SMITTY.]

DAVIS—[*Triumphantly.*] There! Listen to him! Look at him tryin' to git loose! Ain't that proof enough? He knows well we're findin' him out. Listen to me! Love letters, you says, Jack, 's if they couldn't harm nothin'. Listen! I was readin' in some magazine in New York on'y two weeks back how some German spy in Paris was writin' love letters to some woman spy in Switzerland who sent 'em on to Berlin, Germany. To read 'em you wouldn't s'pect nothin'—just mush and all. [*Impressively.*] But they had a way o' doin' it—a damn sneakin' way. They had a piece o' plain paper with pieces cut out of it an' when they puts it on top o' the letter they sees on'y the words what tells them what they wants to know. An' the Frenchies gets beat in a fight all on account o' that letter.

COCKY—[*Awed.*] Gawd blimey! They ain't 'arf smart bleeders!

DAVIS—[*Seeing his audience is again all with him.*] An' even if these letters of his do sound all right they may have what they calls a code. You can't never tell. [*To DRISCOLL, who has finished untying the packet.*] Read one of 'em, Drisc. My eyes is weak.

DRISCOLL—[*Takes the first one out of its envelope and bends down to the lantern with it. He turns up the wick to give him a better light.*] I'm no hand to be readin' but I'll try ut. [*Again there is a muffled groan from SMITTY as he strains at his bonds.*]

DAVIS—[*Gloatingly.*] Listen to him! He knows. Go ahead, Drisc!

DRISCOLL—[*His brow furrowed with concentration.*] Ut begins: Dearest Man—— [*His eyes travel down the page.*] An' thin there's a lot av blarney tellin' him how much she misses him now she's gone away to singin' school—an' how she hopes he'll settle down to rale worrk an' not be sky-larkin' around now that she's away loike he used to before she met up wid him—and ut ends: "I love you betther than anythin' in the worrld. You know that, don't you, dear? But b'fore I can agree to live out my life wid you, you must prove to me that the black shadow—I won't menshun uts hateful name but you know what I mean—which might wreck both our lives, does not exist for you. You can do that, can't you, dear? Don't you see you must for my sake?" [*He pauses for a moment— then adds gruffly.*] Uts signed: "Edith." [*At the sound of the name* SMITTY, *who has stood tensely with his eyes shut as if he were undergoing torture during the reading, makes a muffled sound like a sob and half turns his face to the wall.*]

JACK—[*Sympathetically.*] Hell! What's the use of readin' that stuff even if——

DAVIS—[*Interrupting him sharply.*] Wait! Where's that letter from, Drisc?

DRISCOLL—There's no address on the top av ut.

DAVIS—[*Meaningly.*] What'd I tell you? Look at the postmark, Drisc,—on the envelope.

DRISCOLL—The name that's written is Sidney Davidson, wan hundred an'——

DAVIS—Never mind that. O' course it's a false name. Look at the postmark.

DRISCOLL—There's a furrin stamp on ut by the looks av ut. The mark's blurred so it's hard to read. [*He spells it out laboriously.*] B-e-r—the nixt is an l, I think—i—an' an n.

DAVIS—[*Excitedly.*] Berlin! What did I tell you? I knew them letters was from Germany.

COCKY—[*Shaking his fist in* SMITTY'S *direction.*] Rotten 'ound! [*The others look at* SMITTY *as if this last fact had utterly condemned him in their eyes.*]

DAVIS—Give me the letter, Drisc. Maybe I kin make somethin' out of it. [DRISCOLL *hands the letter to him.*] You go through the others, Drisc, and sing out if you sees anythin' queer. [*He bends over the first letter as if he were determined to figure out its secret meaning.* JACK, COCKY *and* SCOTTY *look over his shoulder with eager curiosity.* DRISCOLL *takes out some of the other letters, running his eyes quickly down the pages. He looks curiously over at* SMITTY *from time to time, and sighs frequently with a puzzled frown.*]

DAVIS—[*Disappointedly.*] I gotter give it up. It's too deep for me, but we'll turn 'em over to the perlice when we docks at Liverpool to look through. This one I got was written a year before the war started, anyway. Find anythin' in yours, Drisc?

DRISCOLL—They're all the same as the first—lovin' blarney, an' how her singin' is doin', and the great things the Dutch teacher says about her voice, an' how glad she is that her Sidney bye is worrkin' harrd an' makin' a man av himself for her sake. [SMITTY *turns his face completely to the wall.*]

DAVIS—[*Disgustedly.*] If we on'y had the code!

Driscoll—[*Taking up the bottom letter.*] Hullo! Here's wan addressed to this ship—s. s. Glencairn, ut says—whin we was in Cape Town sivin months ago—— [*Looking at the postmark.*] Ut's from London.

Davis—[*Eagerly.*] Read it! [*There is another choking groan from* Smitty.]

Driscoll—[*Reads slowly—his voice becomes lower and lower as he goes on.*] Ut begins wid simply the name Sidney Davidson—no dearest or sweetheart to this wan. "Ut is only from your chance meetin' wid Harry—whin you were drunk— that I happen to know where to reach you. So you have run away to sea loike the coward you are because you knew I had found out the truth—the truth you have covered over with your mean little lies all the time I was away in Berlin and blindly trusted you. Very well, you have chosen. You have shown that your drunkenness means more to you than any love or faith av mine. I am sorry— for I loved you, Sidney Davidson—but this is the end. I lave you—the mem'ries; an' if ut is any satisfaction to you I lave you the real-i-zation that you have wrecked my loife as you have wrecked your own. My one remainin' hope is that nivir in God's worrld will I ivir see your face again. Good-by. Edith." [*As he finishes there is a deep silence, broken only by* Smitty's *muffled sobbing. The men cannot look at each other.* Driscoll *holds the rubber bag limply in his hand and some small white object falls out of it and drops noiselessly on the floor. Mechanically* DRISCOLL *leans over and picks it up, and looks at it wonderingly.*]

DAVIS—[*In a dull voice.*] What's that?

DRISCOLL—[*Slowly.*] A bit av a dried-up flower,—a rose, maybe. [*He drops it into the bag and gathers up the letters and puts them back. He replaces the bag in the box, and locks it and puts it back under* SMITTY's *mattress. The others follow him with their eyes. He steps softly over to* SMITTY *and cuts the ropes about his arms and ankles with his sheath knife, and unties the handkerchief over the gag.* SMITTY *does not turn around but covers his face with his hands and leans his head against the wall. His shoulders continue to heave spasmodically but he makes no further sound.*]

DRISCOLL—[*Stalks back to the others—there is a moment of silence, in which each man is in agony with the hopelessness of finding a word he can say— then* DRISCOLL *explodes:*] God stiffen us, are we never goin' to turn in fur a wink av sleep? [*They all start as if awakening from a bad dream and gratefully crawl into their bunks, shoes and all, turning their faces to the wall, and pulling their blankets up over their shoulders.* SCOTTY *tiptoes past* SMITTY *out into the darkness...* DRISCOLL *turns down the light and crawls into his bunk as*

[*The Curtain Falls*]

ILE

A Play In One Act

CHARACTERS

BEN, *the cabin boy*
THE STEWARD
CAPTAIN KEENEY
SLOCUM, *second mate*
MRS. KEENEY
JOE, *a harpooner*
Members of the crew of the steam whaler Atlantic Queen.

ILE

Scene—Captain Keeney's *cabin on board the
steam whaling ship* Atlantic Queen—*a small,
square compartment about eight feet high with
a skylight in the center looking out on the
poop deck. On the left* [*the stern of the
ship*] *a long bench with rough cushions is
built in against the wall. In front of the
bench, a table. Over the bench, several cur-
tained portholes.*

*In the rear, left, a door leading to the cap-
tain's sleeping quarters. To the right of the
door a small organ, looking as if it were brand
new, is placed against the wall.*

*On the right, to the rear, a marble-topped
sideboard. On the sideboard, a woman's sew-
ing basket. Farther forward, a doorway
leading to the companion way, and past the
officer's quarters to the main deck.*

*In the center of the room, a stove. From
the middle of the ceiling a hanging lamp is
suspended. The walls of the cabin are painted
white.*

There is no rolling of the ship, and the light which comes through the skylight is sickly and faint, indicating one of those gray days of calm when ocean and sky are alike dead. The silence is unbroken except for the measured tread of some one walking up and down on the poop deck overhead.

It is nearing two bells—one o'clock—in the afternoon of a day in the year 1895.

At the rise of the curtain there is a moment of intense silence. Then the STEWARD *enters and commences to clear the table of the few dishes which still remain on it after the* CAPTAIN'S *dinner. He is an old, grizzled man dressed in dungaree pants, a sweater, and a woolen cap with ear flaps. His manner is sullen and angry. He stops stacking up the plates and casts a quick glance upward at the skylight; then tiptoes over to the closed door in rear and listens with his ear pressed to the crack. What he hears makes his face darken and he mutters a furious curse. There is a noise from the doorway on the right and he darts back to the table.*

BEN *enters. He is an over-grown, gawky boy with a long, pinched face. He is dressed in sweater, fur cap, etc. His teeth are chattering with the cold and he hurries to the stove, where he stands for a moment shivering, blowing on his hands, slapping them against his sides, on the verge of crying.*

THE STEWARD—[*In relieved tones—seeing who it is.*] Oh, 'tis you, is it? What're ye shiverin' 'bout? Stay by the stove where ye belong and ye'll find no need of chatterin'.

BEN—It's c-c-cold. [*Trying to control his chattering teeth—derisively.*] Who d'ye think it were—the Old Man?

THE STEWARD—[*Makes a threatening move—*BEN *shrinks away.*] None o' your lip, young un, or I'll learn ye. [*More kindly.*] Where was it ye've been all o' the time—the fo'c's'tle?

BEN—Yes.

THE STEWARD—Let the Old Man see ye up for'ard monkeyshinin' with the hands and ye'll get a hidin' ye'll not forget in a hurry.

BEN—Aw, he don't see nothin'. [*A trace of awe in his tones—he glances upward.*] He just walks up and down like he didn't notice nobody—and stares at the ice to the no'the'ard.

THE STEWARD—[*The same tone of awe creeping into his voice.*] He's always starin' at the ice. [*In a sudden rage, shaking his fist at the skylight.*] Ice, ice, ice! Damn him and damn the ice! Holdin' us in for nigh on a year—nothin' to see but ice—stuck in it like a fly in molasses!

BEN—[*Apprehensively.*] Ssshh! He'll hear ye.

THE STEWARD—[*Raging.*] Aye, damn him, and damn the Arctic seas, and damn this stinkin' whalin' ship of his, and damn me for a fool to ever ship on it! [*Subsiding as if realizing the uselessness of this outburst—shaking his head—slowly, with deep conviction.*] He's a hard man—as hard a man as ever sailed the seas.

BEN—[*Solemnly.*] Aye.

THE STEWARD—The two years we all signed up for are done this day. Blessed Christ! Two years o' this dog's life, and no luck in the fishin', and the hands half starved with the food runnin' low, rotten as it is; and not a sign of him turnin' back for home! [*Bitterly.*] Home! I begin to doubt if ever I'll set foot on land again. [*Excitedly.*] What is it he thinks he' goin' to do? Keep us all up here after our time is worked out till the last man of us is starved to death or frozen? We've grub enough hardly to last out the voyage back if we started now. What are the men goin' to do 'bout it? Did ye hear any talk in the fo'c's'tle?

BEN—[*Going over to him—in a half whisper.*] They said if he don't put back south for home to-day they're goin' to mutiny.

THE STEWARD—[*With grim satisfaction.*] Mutiny? Aye, 'tis the only thing they can do; and serve him right after the manner he's treated them—'s if they wern't no better nor dogs.

BEN—The ice is all broke up to s'uth'ard.

They's clear water 's far 's you can see. He ain't got no excuse for not turnin' back for home, the men says.

THE STEWARD—[*Bitterly.*] He won't look no-wheres but no'the'ard where they's only the ice to see. He don't want to see no clear water. All he thinks on is gittin' the ile—'s if it was our fault he ain't had good luck with the whales. [*Shaking his head.*] I think the man's mighty nigh losin' his senses.

BEN—[*Awed.*] D'you really think he's crazy?

THE STEWARD—Aye, it's the punishment o' God on him. Did ye ever hear of a man who wasn't crazy do the things he does? [*Pointing to the door in rear.*] Who but a man that's mad would take his woman—and as sweet a woman as ever was—on a stinkin' whalin' ship to the Arctic seas to be locked in by the rotten ice for nigh on a year, and maybe lose her senses forever—for it's sure she'll never be the same again.

BEN—[*Sadly.*] She useter be awful nice to me before—— [*His eyes grow wide and frightened.*] she got—like she is.

THE STEWARD—Aye, she was good to all of us. 'Twould have been hell on board without her; for he's a hard man—a hard, hard man—a driver if there ever was one. [*With a grim laugh.*] I hope he's satisfied now—drivin' her on till she's near lost her mind. And who could blame her? 'Tis a

God's wonder we're not a ship full of crazed people—with the damned ice all the time, and the quiet so thick you're afraid to hear your own voice.

BEN—[*With a frightened glance toward the door on right.*] She don't never speak to me no more—jest looks at me 's if she didn't know me.

THE STEWARD—She don't know no one—but him. She talks to him—when she does talk—right enough.

BEN—She does nothin' all day long now but sit and sew—and then she cries to herself without makin' no noise. I've seen her.

THE STEWARD—Aye, I could hear her through the door a while back.

BEN—[*Tiptoes over to the door and listens.*] She's cryin' now.

THE STEWARD—[*Furiously—shaking his fist.*] God send his soul to hell for the devil he is! [*There is the noise of some one coming slowly down the companionway stairs.* THE STEWARD *hurries to his stacked up dishes. He is so nervous from fright that he knocks off the top one, which falls and breaks on the floor. He stands aghast, trembling with dread.* BEN *is violently rubbing off the organ with a piece of cloth which he has snatched from his pocket.* CAPTAIN KEENEY *appears in the doorway on right and comes into the cabin, removing his fur cap as he does so. He is a man of about forty, around five-ten in height but looking much shorter on account of the enormous proportions of his shoulders and chest. His face is massive and deeply lined, with gray-blue eyes of a bleak hardness, and a tightly clenched, thin-lipped mouth. His thick hair is long and gray. He is dressed in a heavy blue jacket and blue pants stuffed into his seaboots.*

[He is followed into the cabin by the SECOND MATE, *a rangy six-footer with a lean weather-beaten face. The* MATE *is dressed about the same as the captain. He is a man of thirty or so.]*

KEENEY—*[Comes toward the* STEWARD—*with a stern look on his face. The* STEWARD *is visibly frightened and the stack of dishes rattles in his trembling hands.* KEENEY *draws back his fist and the* STEWARD *shrinks away. The fist is gradually lowered and* KEENEY *speaks slowly.]* 'Twould be like hitting a worm. It is nigh on two bells, Mr. Steward, and this truck not cleared yet.

THE STEWARD—*[Stammering.]* Y-y-yes, sir.

KEENEY—Instead of doin' your rightful work ye've been below here gossipin' old woman's talk with that boy. *[To* BEN, *fiercely.]* Get out o' this, you! Clean up the chart room. *[*BEN *darts past the* MATE *to the open doorway.]* Pick up that dish, MR. STEWARD!

THE STEWARD—*[Doing so with difficulty.]* Yes, sir.

KEENEY—The next dish you break, Mr. Steward,

you take a bath in the Bering Sea at the end of a rope.

THE STEWARD—[*Tremblingly.*] Yes, sir. [*He hurries out. The* SECOND MATE *walks slowly over to the* CAPTAIN.]

MATE—I warn't 'specially anxious the man at the wheel should catch what I wanted to say to you, sir. That's why I asked you to come below.

KEENEY—[*Impatiently.*] Speak your say, Mr. Slocum.

MATE—[*Unconsciously lowering his voice.*] I'm afeard there'll be trouble with the hands by the look o' things. They'll likely turn ugly, every blessed one o' them, if you don't put back. The two years they signed up for is up to-day.

KEENEY—And d'you think you're tellin' me somethin' new, Mr. Slocum? I've felt it in the air this long time past. D'you think I've not seen their ugly looks and the grudgin' way they worked? [*The door in rear is opened and* MRS. KEENEY *stands in the doorway. She is a slight, sweet-faced little woman primly dressed in black. Her eyes are red from weeping and her face drawn and pale. She takes in the cabin with a frightened glance and stands as if fixed to the spot by some nameless dread, clasping and unclasping her hands nervously. The two men turn and look at her.*]

KEENEY—[*With rough tenderness.*] Well, Annie?

MRS. KEENEY—[*As if awakening from a dream.*] David, I—— [*She is silent. The* MATE *starts for the doorway.*]

KEENEY—[*Turning to him—sharply.*] Wait!

MATE—Yes, sir.

KEENEY—D'you want anything, Annie?

MRS. KEENEY—[*After a pause, during which she seems to be endeavoring to collect her thoughts.*] I thought maybe—I'd go up on deck, David, to get a breath of fresh air. [*She stands humbly awaiting his permission. He and the* MATE *exchange a significant glance.*]

KEENEY—It's too cold, Annie. You'd best stay below to-day. There's nothing to look at on deck —but ice.

MRS. KEENEY—[*Monotonously.*] I know—ice, ice, ice! But there's nothing to see down here but these walls. [*She makes a gesture of loathing.*]

KEENEY—You can play the organ, Annie.

MRS. KEENEY—[*Dully.*] I hate the organ. It puts me in mind of home.

KEENEY—[*A touch of resentment in his voice.*] I got it jest for you.

MRS. KEENEY—[*Dully.*] I know. [*She turns away from them and walks slowly to the bench on left. She lifts up one of the curtains and looks through a porthole; then utters an exclamation of joy.*] Ah, water! Clear water! As far as I can see! How good it looks after all these months of ice! [*She turns round to them, her face transfig-ured with joy.*] Ah, now I must go upon deck and look at it, David.

KEENEY—[*Frowning.*] Best not to-day, Annie. Best wait for a day when the sun shines.

MRS. KEENEY—[*Desperately.*] But the sun never shines in this terrible place.

KEENEY—[*A tone of command in his voice.*] Best not to-day, Annie.

MRS. KEENEY—[*Crumbling before this command —abjectly.*] Very well, David. [*She stands there staring straight before her as if in a daze. The two men look at her uneasily.*]

KEENEY—[*Sharply.*] Annie!

MRS. KEENEY—[*Dully.*] Yes, David.

KEENEY—Me and Mr. Slocum has business to talk about—ship's business.

MRS. KEENEY—Very well, David. [*She goes slowly out, rear, and leaves the door three-quarters shut behind her.*]

KEENEY—Best not have her on deck if they's goin' to be any trouble.

MATE—Yes, sir.

KEENEY—And trouble they's goin' to be. I feel it in my bones. [*Takes a revolver from the pocket of his coat and examines it.*] Got your'n?

MATE—Yes, sir.

KEENEY—Not that we'll have to use 'em—not if I know their breed of dog—jest to frighten 'em up a bit. [*Grimly.*] I ain't never been forced to use one yit; and trouble I've had by land and by sea 's long as I kin remember, and will have till my dyin' day, I reckon.

MATE—[*Hesitatingly.*] Then you ain't goin'—to turn back?

KEENEY—Turn back! Mr. Slocum, did you ever hear 'o me pointin' s'uth for home with only a measly four hundred barrel of ile in the hold?

MATE—[*Hastily.*] No, sir—but the grub's gittin' low.

KEENEY—They's enough to last a long time yit, if they're careful with it; and they's plenty o' water.

MATE—They say it's not fit to eat—what's left; and the two years they signed on fur is up to-day. They might make trouble for you in the courts when we git home.

KEENEY—To hell with 'em! Let them make what law trouble they kin. I don't give a damn 'bout the money. I've got to git the ile! [*Glancing sharply at the* MATE.] You ain't turnin' no damned sea lawyer, be you, Mr. Slocum?

MATE—[*Flushing.*] Not by a hell of a sight, sir.

KEENEY—What do the fools want to go home fur now? Their share o' the four hundred barrel wouldn't keep 'em in chewin' terbacco.

MATE—[*Slowly.*] They wants to git back to their folks an' things, I s'pose.

KEENEY—[*Looking at him searchingly.*] 'N you want to turn back, too. [THE MATE *looks down confusedly before his sharp gaze.*] Don't lie, Mr. Slocum. It's writ down plain in your eyes. [*With grim sarcasm.*] I hope, Mr. Slocum, you ain't agoin' to jine the men agin me.

MATE—[*Indignantly.*] That ain't fair, sir, to say sich things.

KEENEY—[*With satisfaction.*] I warn't much afeard o' that, Tom. You been with me nigh on ten year and I've learned ye whalin'. No man kin say I ain't a good master, if I be a hard one.

MATE—I warn't thinkin' of myself, sir—'bout turnin' home, I mean. [*Desperately.*] But Mrs. Keeney, sir—seems like she ain't jest satisfied up here, ailin' like—what with the cold an' bad luck an' the ice an' all.

KEENEY—[*His face clouding—rebukingly but not severely.*] That's my business, Mr. Slocum. I'll thank you to steer a clear course o' that. [*A pause.*] The ice'll break up soon to no'th'ard. I could see it startin' to-day. And when it goes and we git some sun Annie'll perk up. [*Another pause —then he bursts forth:*] It ain't the damned money what's keepin' me up in the Northern seas, Tom. But I can't go back to Homeport with a measly four hundred barrel of ile. I'd die fust. I ain't never come back home in all my days without a full ship. Ain't that truth?

MATE—Yes, sir; but this voyage you been ice-bound, an'——

KEENEY—[*Scornfully.*] And d'you s'pose any of 'em would believe that—any o' them skippers I've beaten voyage after voyage? Can't you hear 'em laughin' and sneerin'—Tibbots 'n' Harris 'n' Simms and the rest—and all o' Homeport makin' fun o' me? "Dave Keeney what boasts he's the best whalin' skipper out o' Homeport comin' back with a measly four hundred barrel of ile?" [*The thought of this drives him into a frenzy, and he smashes his fist down on the marble top of the sideboard.*] Hell! I got to git the ile, I tell you. How could I figger on this ice? It's never been so bad before in the thirty year I been acomin' here. And now it's breakin' up. In a couple o' days it'll be all gone. And they's whale here, plenty of 'em. I know they is and I ain't never gone wrong yit. I got to git the ile! I got to git it in spite of all hell, and by God, I ain't agoin' home till I do git it! [*There is the sound of subdued sobbing from the door in rear. The two men stand silent for a moment, listening. Then* KEENEY *goes over to the door and looks in. He hesitates for a moment as if he were going to enter—then closes the door softly.* JOE, *the harpooner, an enormous six-footer with a battered, ugly face, enters from right and stands waiting for the captain to notice him.*]

KEENEY—[*Turning and seeing him.*] Don't be

standin' there like a gawk, Harpooner. Speak up!

Joe—[*Confusedly.*] We want—the men, sir— they wants to send a depitation aft to have a word with you.

Keeney—[*Furiously.*] Tell 'em to go to—— [*Checks himself and continues grimly.*] Tell 'em to come. I'll see 'em.

Joe—Aye, aye, sir. [*He goes out.*]

Keeney—[*With a grim smile.*] Here it comes, the trouble you spoke of, Mr. Slocum, and we'll make short shift of it. It's better to crush such things at the start than let them make headway.

Mate—[*Worriedly.*] Shall I wake up the First and Fourth, sir? We might need their help.

Keeney—No, let them sleep. I'm well able to handle this alone, Mr. Slocum. [*There is the shuffling of footsteps from outside and five of the crew crowd into the cabin, led by* Joe. *All are dressed alike—sweaters, seaboots, etc. They glance uneasily at the* Captain, *twirling their fur caps in their hands.*]

Keeney—[*After a pause.*] Well? Who's to speak fur ye?

Joe—[*Stepping forward with an air of bravado.*] I be.

Keeney—[*Eyeing him up and down coldly.*] So you be. Then speak your say and be quick about it.

Joe—[*Trying not to wilt before the* Captain's

glance and avoiding his eyes.] The time we signed up for is done to-day.

KEENEY—[*Icily.*] You're tellin' me nothin' I don't know.

JOE—You ain't pintin' fur home yit, far 's we kin see.

KEENEY—No, and I ain't agoin' to till this ship is full of ile.

JOE—You can't go no further no'the with the ice afore ye.

KEENEY—The ice is breaking up.

JOE—[*After a slight pause during which the others mumble angrily to one another.*] The grub we're gittin' now is rotten.

KEENEY—It's good enough fur ye. Better men than ye are have eaten worse. [*There is a chorus of angry exclamations from the crowd.*]

JOE—[*Encouraged by this support.*] We ain't agoin' to work no more less you puts back for home.

KEENEY—[*Fiercely.*] You ain't, ain't you?

JOE—No; and the law courts'll say we was right.

KEENEY—To hell with your law courts! We're at sea now and I'm the law on this ship. [*Edging up toward the harpooner.*] And every mother's son of you what don't obey orders goes in irons. [*There are more angry exclamations from the crew. MRS. KEENEY appears in the doorway in rear and looks on with startled eyes. None of the men notice her.*]

JOE—[*With bravado.*] Then we're agoin' to

mutiny and take the old hooker home ourselves. Ain't we, boys? [*As he turns his head to look at the others,* KEENEY's *fist shoots out to the side of his jaw.* JOE *goes down in a heap and lies there.* MRS. KEENEY *gives a shriek and hides her face in her hands. The men pull out their sheath knives and start a rush, but stop when they find themselves confronted by the revolvers of* KEENEY *and the* MATE.]

KEENEY—[*His eyes and voice snapping.*] Hold still! [*The men stand huddled together in a sullen silence.* KEENEY's *voice is full of mockery.*] You've found out it ain't safe to mutiny on this ship, ain't you? And now git for'ard where ye belong, and—— [*He gives* JOE's *body a contemptuous kick.*] Drag him with you. And remember the first man of ye I see shirkin' I'll shoot dead as sure as there's a sea under us, and you can tell the rest the same. Git for'ard now! Quick! [*The men leave in cowed silence, carrying* JOE *with them.* KEENEY *turns to the* MATE *with a short laugh and puts his revolver back in his pocket.*] Best get up on deck, Mr. Slocum, and see to it they don't try none of their skulkin' tricks. We'll have to keep an eye peeled from now on. I know 'em.

MATE—Yes, sir. [*He goes out, right.* KEENEY *hears his wife's hysterical weeping and turns around in surprise—then walks slowly to her side.*]

KEENEY—[*Putting an arm around her shoulder*

—*with gruff tenderness.*] There, there, Annie.
Don't be afeard. It's all past and gone.

MRS. KEENEY—[*Shrinking away from him.*] Oh,
I can't bear it! I can't bear it any longer!

KEENEY—[*Gently.*] Can't bear what, Annie?

MRS. KEENEY—[*Hysterically.*] All this horrible
brutality, and these brutes of men, and this terrible
ship, and this prison cell of a room, and the ice all
around, and the silence. [*After this outburst she
calms down and wipes her eyes with her handkerchief.*]

KEENEY—[*After a pause during which he looks
down at her with a puzzled frown.*] Remember, I
warn't hankerin' to have you come on this voyage,
Annie.

MRS. KEENEY—I wanted to be with you, David,
don't you see? I didn't want to wait back there
in the house all alone as I've been doing these last
six years since we were married—waiting, and
watching, and fearing—with nothing to keep my
mind occupied—not able to go back teaching school
on account of being Dave Keeney's wife. I used to
dream of sailing on the great, wide, glorious ocean.
I wanted to be by your side in the danger and vig-
orous life of it all. I wanted to see you the hero
they make you out to be in Homeport. And instead—— [*Her voice grows tremulous.*] All I
find is ice and cold—and brutality! [*Her voice
breaks.*]

Keeney—I warned you what it'd be, Annie. "Whalin' ain't no ladies' tea party," I says to you, and "you better stay to home where you've got all your woman's comforts." [*Shaking his head.*] But you was so set on it.

Mrs. Keeney—[*Wearily.*] Oh, I know it isn't your fault, David. You see, I didn't believe you. I guess I was dreaming about the old Vikings in the story books and I thought you were one of them.

Keeney—[*Protestingly.*] I done my best to make it as cozy and comfortable as could be. [Mrs. Keeney *looks around her in wild scorn.*] I even sent to the city for that organ for ye, thinkin' it might be soothin' to ye to be playin' it times when they was calms and things was dull like.

Mrs. Keeney—[*Wearily.*] Yes, you were very kind, David. I know that. [*She goes to left and lifts the curtains from the porthole and looks out—then suddenly bursts forth:*] I won't stand it—I can't stand it—pent up by these walls like a prisoner. [*She runs over to him and throws her arms around him, weeping. He puts his arm protectingly over her shoulders.*] Take me away from here, David! If I don't get away from here, out of this terrible ship, I'll go mad! Take me home, David! I can't think any more. I feel as if the cold and the silence were crushing down on my brain. I'm afraid. Take me home!

Keeney—[*Holds her at arm's length and looks*

at her face anxiously.] Best go to bed, Annie. You ain't yourself. You got fever. Your eyes look so strange like. I ain't never seen you look this way before.

MRS. KEENEY—[*Laughing hysterically.*] It's the ice and the cold and the silence—they'd make any one look strange.

KEENEY—[*Soothingly.*] In a month or two, with good luck, three at the most, I'll have her filled with ile and then we'll give her everything she'll stand and pint for home.

MRS. KEENEY—But we can't wait for that—I can't wait. I want to get home. And the men won't wait. They want to get home. It's cruel, it's brutal for you to keep them. You must sail back. You've got no excuse. There's clear water to the south now. If you've a heart at all you've got to turn back.

KEENEY—[*Harshly.*] I can't, Annie.

MRS. KEENEY—Why can't you?

KEENEY—A woman couldn't rightly understand my reason.

MRS. KEENEY—[*Wildly.*] Because it's a stupid, stubborn reason. Oh, I heard you talking with the second mate. You're afraid the other captains will sneer at you because you didn't come back with a full ship. You want to live up to your silly reputation even if you do have to beat and starve men and drive me mad to do it.

KEENEY—[*His jaw set stubbornly.*] It ain't
that, Annie. Them skippers would never dare sneer
to my face. It ain't so much what any one'd say—
but—— [*He hesitates, struggling to express his
meaning.*] You see—I've always done it—since
my first voyage as skipper. I always come back—
with a full ship—and—it don't seem right not to—
somehow. I been always first whalin' skipper out o'
Homeport, and—— Don't you see my meanin',
Annie? [*He glances at her. She is not looking at
him but staring dully in front of her, not hearing
a word he is saying.*] Annie! [*She comes to herself with a start.*] Best turn in, Annie, there's a
good woman. You ain't well.

MRS. KEENEY—[*Resisting his attempts to guide
her to the door in rear.*] David! Won't you please
turn back?

KEENEY—[*Gently.*] I can't, Annie—not yet
awhile. You don't see my meanin'. I got to git the
ile.

MRS. KEENEY—It'd be different if you needed the
money, but you don't. You've got more than plenty.

KEENEY—[*Impatiently.*] It ain't the money I'm
thinkin' of. D'you think I'm as mean as that?

MRS. KEENEY—[*Dully.*] No—I don't know—I
can't understand—— [*Intensely.*] Oh, I want to
be home in the old house once more and see my own
kitchen again, and hear a woman's voice talking to
me and be able to talk to her. Two years! It

seems so long ago—as if I'd been dead and could never go back.

KEENEY—[*Worried by her strange tone and the far-away look in her eyes.*] Best go to bed, Annie. You ain't well.

MRS. KEENEY—[*Not appearing to hear him.*] I used to be lonely when you were away. I used to think Homeport was a stupid, monotonous place. Then I used to go down on the beach, especially when it was windy and the breakers were rolling in, and I'd dream of the fine free life you must be leading. [*She gives a laugh which is half a sob.*] I used to love the sea then. [*She pauses; then continues with slow intensity:*] But now—I don't ever want to see the sea again.

KEENEY—[*Thinking to humor her.*] 'Tis no fit place for a woman, that's sure. I was a fool to bring ye.

MRS. KEENEY—[*After a pause—passing her hand over her eyes with a gesture of pathetic weariness.*] How long would it take us to reach home—if we started now?

KEENEY—[*Frowning.*] 'Bout two months, I reckon, Annie, with fair luck.

MRS. KEENEY—[*Counts on her fingers—then murmurs with a rapt smile.*] That would be August, the latter part of August, wouldn't it? It was on the twenty-fifth of August we were married, David, wasn't it?

KEENEY—[*Trying to conceal the fact that her memories have moved him—gruffly.*] Don't *you* remember?

MRS. KEENEY—[*Vaguely—again passes her hand over her eyes.*] My memory is leaving me—up here in the ice. It was so long ago. [*A pause—then she smiles dreamily.*] It's June now. The lilacs will be all in bloom in the front yard—and the climbing roses on the trellis to the side of the house— they're budding. [*She suddenly covers her face with her hands and commences to sob.*]

KEENEY—[*Disturbed.*] Go in and rest, Annie. You're all wore out cryin' over what can't be helped.

MRS. KEENEY—[*Suddenly throwing her arms around his neck and clinging to him.*] You love me, don't you, David?

KEENEY—[*In amazed embarrassment at this outburst.*] Love you? Why d'you ask me such a question, Annie?

MRS. KEENEY—[*Shaking him—fiercely.*] But you do, don't you, David? Tell me!

KEENEY—I'm your husband, Annie, and you're my wife. Could there be aught but love between us after all these years?

MRS. KEENEY—[*Shaking him again—still more fiercely.*] Then you do love me. Say it!

KEENEY—[*Simply.*] I do, Annie.

MRS. KEENEY—[*Gives a sigh of relief—her hands drop to her sides. Keeney regards her anxiously.*]

She passes her hand across her eyes and murmurs half to herself:] I sometimes think if we could only have had a child. [KEENEY *turns away from her, deeply moved. She grabs his arm and turns him around to face her—intensely.*] And I've always been a good wife to you, haven't I, David?

KEENEY—[*His voice betraying his emotion.*] No man has ever had a better, Annie.

MRS. KEENEY—And I've never asked for much from you, have I, David? Have I?

KEENEY—You know you could have all I got the power to give ye, Annie.

MRS. KEENEY—[*Wildly.*] Then do this this once for my sake, for God's sake—take me home! It's killing me, this life—the brutality and cold and horror of it. I'm going mad. I can feel the threat in the air. I can hear the silence threatening me—day after gray day and every day the same. I can't bear it. [*Sobbing.*] I'll go mad, I know I will. Take me home, David, if you love me as you say. I'm afraid. For the love of God, take me home! [*She throws her arms around him, weeping against his shoulder. His face betrays the tremendous struggle going on within him. He holds her out at arm's length, his expression softening. For a moment his shoulders sag, he becomes old, his iron spirit weakens as he looks at her tear-stained face.*]

KEENEY—[*Dragging out the words with an ef-*

fort.] I'll do it, Annie—for your sake—if you say it's needful for ye.

MRS. KEENEY—[*With wild joy—kissing him.*] God bless you for that, David! [*He turns away from her silently and walks toward the companionway. Just at that moment there is a clatter of footsteps on the stairs and the* SECOND MATE *enters the cabin.*]

MATE—[*Excitedly.*] The ice is breakin' up to no'the'ard, sir. There's a clear passage through the floe, and clear water beyond, the lookout says. [KEENEY *straightens himself like a man coming out of a trance.* MRS. KEENEY *looks at the* MATE *with terrified eyes.*]

KEENEY—[*Dazedly—trying to collect his thoughts.*] A clear passage? To no'the'ard?

MATE—Yes, sir.

KEENEY—[*His voice suddenly grim with determination.*] Then get her ready and we'll drive her through.

MATE—Aye, aye, sir.

MRS. KEENEY—[*Appealingly.*] David!

KEENEY—[*Not heeding her.*] Will the men turn to willin' or must we drag 'em out?

MATE—They'll turn to willin' enough. You put the fear o' God into 'em, sir. They're meek as lambs.

KEENEY—Then drive 'em—both watches. [*With*

grim determination.] They's whale t'other side o' this floe and we're going to git 'em.

MATE—Aye, aye, sir. [*He goes out hurriedly. A moment later there is the sound of scuffling feet from the deck outside and the* MATE'S *voice shouting orders.*]

KEENEY—[*Speaking aloud to himself—derisively.*] And I was agoin' home like a yaller dog!

MRS. KEENEY—[*Imploringly.*] David!

KEENEY—[*Sternly.*] Woman, you ain't adoin' right when you meddle in men's business and weaken 'em. You can't know my feelin's. I got to prove a man to be a good husband for ye to take pride in. I got to git the ile, I tell ye.

MRS. KEENEY—[*Supplicatingly.*] David! Aren't you going home?

KEENEY—[*Ignoring this question — commandingly.*] You ain't well. Go and lay down a mite. [*He starts for the door.*] I got to git on deck. [*He goes out. She cries after him in anguish:*] David! [*A pause. She passes her hand across her eyes—then commences to laugh hysterically and goes to the organ. She sits down and starts to play wildly an old hymn.* KEENEY *reënters from the doorway to the deck and stands looking at her angrily. He comes over and grabs her roughly by the shoulder.*]

KEENEY—Woman, what foolish mockin' is this? [*She laughs wildly and he starts back from her in alarm.*] Annie! What is it? [*She doesn't answer him.* KEENEY'S *voice trembles.*] Don't you know me, Annie? [*He puts both hands on her shoulders and turns her around so that he can look into her eyes. She stares up at him with a stupid expression, a vague smile on her lips. He stumbles away from her, and she commences softly to play the organ again.*]

KEENEY—[*Swallowing hard—in a hoarse whisper, as if he had difficulty in speaking.*] You said —you was a-goin' mad—God! [*A long wail is heard from the deck above.*] Ah bl-o-o-o-ow! [*A moment later the* MATE'S *face appears through the skylight. He cannot see* MRS. KEENEY.]

MATE—[*In great excitement.*] Whales, sir—a whole school of 'em—off the star'b'd quarter 'bout five mile away—big ones!

KEENEY—[*Galvanized into action.*] Are you lowerin' the boats?

MATE—Yes, sir.

KEENEY—[*With grim decision.*] I'm a-comin' with ye.

MATE—Aye, aye, sir. [*Jubilantly.*] You'll git the ile now right enough, sir. [*His head is withdrawn and he can be heard shouting orders.*]

KEENEY—[*Turning to his wife.*] Annie! Did you hear him? I'll git the ile. [*She doesn't answer or seem to know he is there. He gives a hard laugh, which is almost a groan.*] I know you're foolin' me,

Annie. You ain't out of your mind—[*Anxiously.*]
be you? I'll git the ile now right enough—jest a little
while longer, Annie—then we'll turn hom'ard. I
can't turn back now, you see that, don't ye? I've
got to git the ile. [*In sudden terror.*] Answer me!
You ain't mad, be you? [*She keeps on playing the
organ, but makes no reply. The* MATE's *face appears again through the skylight.*]

MATE—All ready, sir. [KEENEY *turns his back
on his wife and strides to the doorway, where he
stands for a moment and looks back at her in
anguish, fighting to control his feelings.*]

MATE—Comin', sir?

KEENEY—[*His face suddenly grown hard with
determination.*] Aye. [*He turns abruptly and goes
out.* MRS. KEENEY *does not appear to notice his
departure. Her whole attention seems centered in
the organ. She sits with half-closed eyes, her body
swaying a little from side to side to the rhythm of
the hymn. Her fingers move faster and faster and
she is playing wildly and discordantly as*

[*The Curtain Falls*]

WHERE THE CROSS IS MADE

A Play In One Act

Captain Isaiah Bartlett
Nat Bartlett, *his son*
Sue Bartlett, *his daughter*
Doctor Higgins
Silas Horne, *mate*
Cates, *bo'sun*   } *of the schooner* Mary
Jimmy Kanaka, *harpooner*   Allen

WHERE THE CROSS IS MADE

SCENE—*Captain Bartlett's "cabin"—a room erected as a lookout post at the top of his house situated on a high point of land on the California coast. The inside of the compartment is fitted up like the captain's cabin of a deep-sea sailing vessel. On the left, forward, a porthole. Farther back, the stairs of the companionway. Still farther, two more portholes. In the rear, left, a marble-topped sideboard with a ship's lantern on it. In the rear, center, a door opening on stairs which lead to the lower house. A cot with a blanket is placed against the wall to the right of the door. In the right wall, five portholes. Directly under them, a wooden bench. In front of the bench, a long table with two straight-backed chairs, one in front, the other to the left of it. A cheap, dark-colored rug is on the floor. In the ceiling, midway from front to rear, a skylight extending from opposite the door to above the left edge of the table. In the right extremity of the skylight is placed a floating ship's compass. The light from the binnacle sheds over this from above and seeps down into the room, casting a vague globular shadow of the compass on the floor.*

The time is an early hour of a clear windy night in the fall of the year 1900. Moonlight, winnowed by the wind which moans in the stubborn angles of the old house, creeps wearily in through the portholes and rests like tired dust in circular patches upon the floor and table. An insistent monotone of thundering surf, muffled and far-off, is borne upward from the beach below.

After the curtain rises the door in the rear is opened slowly and the head and shoulders of NAT BARTLETT *appear over the sill. He casts a quick glance about the room, and seeing no one there, ascends the remaining steps and enters. He makes a sign to some one in the darkness beneath:* "All right, Doctor." DOCTOR HIGGINS *follows him into the room and, closing the door, stands looking with great curiosity around him. He is a slight, medium-sized professional-looking man of about thirty-five.* NAT BARTLETT *is very tall, gaunt, and loose-framed. His right arm has been amputated at the shoulder and the sleeve on that side of the heavy mackinaw he wears hangs flabbily or flaps against his body as he moves. He ap-*

pears much older than his thirty years. His shoulders have a weary stoop as if worn down by the burden of his massive head with its heavy shock of tangled black hair. His face is long, bony, and sallow, with deep-set black eyes, a large aquiline nose, a wide thin-lipped mouth shadowed by an unkempt bristle of mustache. His voice is low and deep with a penetrating, hollow, metallic quality. In addition to the mackinaw, he wears corduroy trousers stuffed down into high laced boots.

NAT—Can you see, Doctor?

HIGGINS—[*In the too-casual tones which betray an inward uneasiness.*] Yes—perfectly—don't trouble. The moonlight is so bright——

NAT—Luckily. [*Walking slowly toward the table.*] He doesn't want any light—lately—only the one from the binnacle there.

HIGGINS—He? Ah—you mean your father?

NAT—[*Impatiently.*] Who else?

HIGGINS—[*A bit startled—gazing around him in embarrassment.*] I suppose this is all meant to be like a ship's cabin?

NAT—Yes—as I warned you.

HIGGINS—[*In surprise.*] Warned me? Why, warned? I think it's very natural—and interesting —this whim of his.

NAT—[*Meaningly.*] Interesting, it may be.

HIGGINS—And he lives up here, you said—never comes down?

NAT—Never—for the past three years. My sister brings his food up to him. [*He sits down in the chair to the left of the table.*] There's a lantern on the sideboard there, Doctor. Bring it over and sit down. We'll make a light. I'll ask your pardon for bringing you to this room on the roof—but—no one'll hear us here; and by seeing for yourself the mad way he lives—— Understand that I want you to get all the facts—just that, facts!—and for that light is necessary. Without that—they become dreams up here—dreams, Doctor.

HIGGINS—[*With a relieved smile carries over the lantern.*] It is a trifle spooky.

NAT—[*Not seeming to notice this remark.*] He won't take any note of this light. His eyes are too busy—out there. [*He flings his left arm in a wide gesture seaward.*] And if he does notice—well, let him come down. You're bound to see him sooner or later. [*He scratches a match and lights the lantern.*]

HIGGINS—Where is—he?

NAT—[*Pointing upward.*] Up on the poop. Sit down, man! He'll not come—yet awhile.

HIGGINS—[*Sitting gingerly on the chair in front of table.*] Then he has the roof too rigged up like a ship?

NAT—I told you he had. Like a deck, yes. A

wheel, compass, binnacle light, the companionway there [*He points.*], a bridge to pace up and down on —*and keep watch.* If the wind wasn't so high you'd hear him now—back and forth—all the live-long night. [*With a sudden harshness.*] Didn't I tell you he's mad?

HIGGINS—[*With a professional air.*] That was nothing new. I've heard that about him from all sides since I first came to the asylum yonder. You say he only walks at night—up there?

NAT—Only at night, yes. [*Grimly.*] The things he wants to see can't be made out in daylight— dreams and such.

HIGGINS—But just what is he trying to see? Does any one know? Does he tell?

NAT—[*Impatiently.*] Why, every one knows what Father looks for, man! The ship, of course.

HIGGINS—What ship?

NAT—His ship—the Mary Allen—named for my dead mother.

HIGGINS—But—I don't understand—— Is the ship long overdue—or what?

NAT—Lost in a hurricane off the Celebes with all on board—three years ago!

HIGGINS—[*Wonderingly.*] Ah. [*After a pause.*] But your father still clings to a doubt——

NAT—There is no doubt for him or any one else to cling to. She was sighted bottom up, a complete wreck, by the whaler John Slocum. That was two weeks after the storm. They sent a boat out to read her name.

HIGGINS—And hasn't your father ever heard——

NAT—He was the first to hear, naturally. Oh, he *knows* right enough, if that's what you're driving at. [*He bends toward the doctor—intensely.*] He *knows*, Doctor, he *knows*—but he won't *believe*. He can't—and keep living.

HIGGINS—[*Impatiently.*] Come, Mr. Bartlett, let's get down to brass tacks. You didn't drag me up here to make things more obscure, did you? Let's have the facts you spoke of. I'll need them to give sympathetic treatment to his case when we get him to the asylum.

NAT—[*Anxiously—lowering his voice.*] And you'll come to take him away to-night—for sure?

HIGGINS—Twenty minutes after I leave here I'll be back in the car. That's positive.

NAT—And you know your way through the house?

HIGGINS—Certainly, I remember—but I don't see——

NAT—The outside door will be left open for you. You must come right up. My sister and I will be here—with him. And you understand—— Neither of us knows anything about this. The authorities have been complained to—not by us, mind—but by some one. He must never know——

Higgins—Yes, yes—but still I don't—— Is he liable to prove violent?

Nat—No—no. He's quiet always—too quiet; but he might do something—anything—if he knows——

Higgins—Rely on me not to tell him, then; but I'll bring along two attendants in case—— [*He breaks off and continues in matter-of-fact tones.*] And now for the facts in this case, if you don't mind, Mr. Bartlett.

Nat—[*Shaking his head—moodily.*] There are cases where facts—— Well, here goes—the brass tacks. My father was a whaling captain as his father before him. The last trip he made was seven years ago. He expected to be gone two years. It was four before we saw him again. His ship had been wrecked in the Indian Ocean. He and six others managed to reach a small island on the fringe of the Archipelago—an island barren as hell, Doctor—after seven days in an open boat. The rest of the whaling crew never were heard from again—gone to the sharks. Of the six who reached the island with my father only three were alive when a fleet of Malay canoes picked them up, mad from thirst and starvation, the four of them. These four men finally reached Frisco. [*With great emphasis.*] They were my father; Silas Horne, the mate; Cates, the bo'sun, and Jimmy Kanaka, a Hawaiian harpooner. Those four! [*With a forced laugh.*]

There are facts for you. It was all in the papers at the time—my father's story.

HIGGINS—But what of the other three who were on the island?

NAT—[*Harshly.*] Died of exposure, perhaps. Mad and jumped into the sea, perhaps. That was the told story. Another was whispered—killed and eaten, perhaps! But gone—vanished—that, undeniably. That was the fact. For the rest—who knows? And what does it matter?

HIGGINS—[*With a shudder.*] I should think it would matter—a lot.

NAT—[*Fiercely.*] We're dealing with facts, Doctor! [*With a laugh.*] And here are some more for you. My father brought the three down to this house with him—Horne and Cates and Jimmy Kanaka. We hardly recognized my father. He had been through hell and looked it. His hair was white. But you'll see for yourself—soon. And the others —they were all a bit queer, too—mad, if you will. [*He laughs again.*] So much for the facts, Doctor. They leave off there and the dreams begin.

HIGGINS—[*Doubtfully.*] It would seem—the facts are enough.

NAT—Wait. [*He resumes deliberately.*] One day my father sent for me and in the presence of the others told me the dream. I was to be heir to the secret. Their second day on the island, he said, they discovered in a sheltered inlet the rotten, waterlogged hulk of a Malay prau—a proper war prau such as the pirates used to use. She had been there rotting—God knows how long. The crew had vanished—God knows where, for there was no sign on the island that man had ever touched there. The Kanakas went over the prau—they're devils for staying under water, you know—and they found— in two chests—[*he leans back in his chair and smiles ironically*]—Guess what, Doctor?

HIGGINS—[*With an answering smile.*] Treasure, of course.

NAT—[*Leaning forward and pointing his finger accusingly at the other.*] You see! The root of belief is in you, too! [*Then he leans back with a hollow chuckle.*] Why, yes. Treasure, to be sure. What else? They landed it and—you can guess the rest, too—diamonds, emeralds, gold ornaments— innumerable, of course. Why limit the stuff of dreams? Ha-ha! [*He laughs sardonically as if mocking himself.*]

HIGGINS—[*Deeply interested.*] And then?

NAT—They began to go mad—hunger, thirst, and the rest—and they began to forget. Oh, they forgot a lot, and lucky for them they did, probably. But my father realizing, as he told me, what was happening to them, insisted that while they still knew what they were doing they should—guess again now, Doctor. Ha-ha!

HIGGINS—Bury the treasure?

NAT—[*Ironically.*] Simple, isn't it? Ha-ha. And then they made a map—the same old dream, you see—with a charred stick, and my father had care of it. They were picked up soon after, mad as hatters, as I have told you, by some Malays. [*He drops his mocking and adopts a calm, deliberate tone again.*] But the map isn't a dream, Doctor. We're coming back to facts again. [*He reaches into the pocket of his mackinaw and pulls out a crumpled paper.*] Here. [*He spreads it out on the table.*]

HIGGINS—[*Craning his neck eagerly.*] Dammit! This is interesting. The treasure, I suppose, is where——

NAT—Where the cross is made.

HIGGINS—And here are the signatures, I see. And that sign?

NAT—Jimmy Kanaka's. He couldn't write.

HIGGINS—And below? That's yours, isn't it?

NAT—As heir to the secret, yes. We all signed it here the morning the Mary Allen, the schooner my father had mortgaged this house to fit out, set sail to bring back the treasure. Ha-ha.

HIGGINS—The ship he's still looking for—that was lost three years ago?

NAT—The Mary Allen, yes. The other three men sailed away on her. Only father and the mate knew the approximate location of the island—and I—as heir. It's—— [*He hesitates, frowning.*] No

matter. I'll keep the mad secret. My father wanted
to go with them—but my mother was dying. I
dared not go either.

HIGGINS—Then you wanted to go? You believed
in the treasure then?

NAT—Of course. Ha-ha. How could I help it?
I believed until my mother's death. Then *he* became mad, entirely mad. He built this cabin—to
wait in—and he suspected my growing doubt as time
went on. So, as final proof, he gave me a thing he
had kept hidden from them all—a sample of the
richest of the treasure. Ha-ha. Behold! [*He takes
from his pocket a heavy bracelet thickly studded
with stones and throws it on the table near the lantern.*]

HIGGINS—[*Picking it up with eager curiosity—
as if in spite of himself.*] Real jewels?

NAT—Ha-ha! You want to believe, too. No—
paste and brass—Malay ornaments.

HIGGINS—You had it looked over?

NAT—Like a fool, yes. [*He puts it back in his
pocket and shakes his head as if throwing off a
burden.*] Now you know why he's mad—waiting
for that ship—and why in the end I had to ask
you to take him away where he'll be safe. The
mortgage—the price of that ship—is to be fore-
closed. We have to move, my sister and I. We
can't take him with us. She is to be married soon.
Perhaps away from the sight of the sea he may——

HIGGINS—[*Perfunctorily.*]   Let's hope for the best. And I fully appreciate your position. [*He gets up, smiling.*] And thank you for the interesting story. I'll know how to humor him when he raves about treasure.

NAT—[*Somberly.*]   He is quiet always—too quiet. He only walks to and fro—watching——

HIGGINS—Well, I must go. You think it's best to take him to-night?

NAT [*Persuasively.*]   Yes, Doctor. The neighbors—they're far away but—for my sister's sake—you understand.

HIGGINS—I see. It must be hard on her—this sort of thing—Well.—[*He goes to the door, which* NAT *opens for him.*] I'll return presently. [*He starts to descend.*]

NAT—[*Urgently.*]   Don't fail us, Doctor. And come right up. He'll be here. [*He closes the door and tiptoes carefully to the companionway. He ascends it a few steps and remains for a moment listening for some sound from above. Then he goes over to the table, turning the lantern very low, and sits down, resting his elbows, his chin on his hands, staring somberly before him. The door in the rear is slowly opened. It creaks slightly and* NAT *jumps to his feet—in a thick voice of terror.*]   Who's there? [*The door swings wide open, revealing* SUE BARTLETT. *She ascends into the room and shuts the door behind her. She is a tall, slender woman of twenty-five, with a pale, sad face framed in a mass of dark red hair. This hair furnishes the only touch of color about her. Her full lips are pale; the blue of her wistful wide eyes is fading into a twilight gray. Her voice is low and melancholy. She wears a dark wrapper and slippers.*]

Sue—[*Stands and looks at her brother accusingly.*] It's only I. What are you afraid of?

Nat—[*Averts his eyes and sinks back on his chair again.*] Nothing. I didn't know—I thought you were in your room.

Sue—[*Comes to the table.*] I was reading. Then I heard some one come down the stairs and go out. Who was it? [*With sudden terror.*] It wasn't—Father?

Nat—No. He's up there—watching—as he always is.

Sue—[*Sitting down—insistently.*] Who was it?

Nat—[*Evasively.*] A man—I know.

Sue—What man? What is he? You're holding something back. Tell me.

Nat—[*Raising his eyes defiantly.*] A doctor.

Sue—[*Alarmed*] Oh! [*With quick intuition.*] You brought him up here—so that I wouldn't know!

Nat—[*Doggedly.*] No. I took him up here to see how things were—to ask him about Father.

Sue—[*As if afraid of the answer she will get.*]

Is he one of them—from the asylum? Oh, Nat, you haven't——

NAT—[*Interrupting her—hoarsely.*]   No, no! Be still.

SUE—That would be—the last horror.

NAT—[*Defiantly.*]   Why? You always say that. What could be more horrible than things as they are? I believe—it would be better for him—away —where he couldn't see the sea. He'll forget his mad idea of waiting for a lost ship and a treasure that never was. [*As if trying to convince himself —vehemently.*] I believe this!

SUE—[*Reproachfully.*]   You don't, Nat. You know he'd die if he hadn't the sea to live with.

NAT—[*Bitterly.*]   And you know old Smith will foreclose the mortgage. Is that nothing? We cannot pay. He came yesterday and talked with me. He knows the place is his—to all purposes. He talked as if we were merely his tenants, curse him! And he swore he'd foreclose immediately unless——

SUE—[*Eagerly.*]   What?

NAT—[*In a hard voice.*]   Unless we have— Father—taken away.

SUE—[*In anguish.*]   Oh! But why, why? What is Father to him?

NAT—The value of the property—our home which is his, Smith's. The neighbors are afraid. They pass by on the road at nights coming back to their farms from the town. They see *him* up there walking back and forth—waving his arms against the sky. They're afraid. They talk of a complaint. They say for his own good he must be taken away. They even whisper the house is haunted. Old Smith is afraid of his property. He thinks that *he* may set fire to the house—do anything——

SUE [*Despairingly.*] But you told him how foolish that was, didn't you? That Father is quiet, always quiet.

NAT—What's the use of telling—when they believe—when they're afraid? [SUE *hides her face in her hands—a pause—*NAT *whispers hoarsely:*] I've been afraid myself—at times.

SUE—Oh, Nat! Of what?

NAT—[*Violently.*] Oh, him and the sea he calls to! Of the damned sea he forced me on as a boy— the sea that robbed me of my arm and made me the broken thing I am!

SUE [*Pleadingly.*] You can't blame Father— for your misfortune.

NAT—He took me from school and forced me on his ship, didn't he? What would I have been now but an ignorant sailor like him if he had had his way? No. It's the sea I should not blame, that foiled him by taking my arm and then throwing me ashore—another one of *his* wrecks!

SUE—[*With a sob.*] You're bitter, Nat—and hard. It was so long ago. Why can't you forget?

NAT—[*Bitterly.*] Forget! You can talk!

When Tom comes home from this voyage you'll be married and out of this with life before you—a captain's wife as our mother was. I wish you joy.

SUE—[*Supplicatingly.*] And you'll come with us, Nat—and father, too—and then——

NAT—Would you saddle your young husband with a madman and a cripple? [*Fiercely.*] No, no, not I! [*Vindictively.*] And not him, either! [*With sudden meaning—deliberately.*] I've got to stay here. My book is three-fourths done—my book that will set me free! But I know, I feel, as sure as I stand here living before you, that I must finish it here. It could not live for me outside of this house where it was born. [*Staring at her fixedly.*] So I will stay—in spite of hell! [SUE *sobs hopelessly. After a pause he continues:*] Old Smith told me I could live here indefinitely without paying —as caretaker—if——

SUE—[*Fearfully—like a whispered echo.*] If?

NAT—[*Staring at her—in a hard voice.*] If I have *him* sent—where he'll no longer harm himself —nor others.

SUE—[*With horrified dread.*] No—no, Nat! For our dead mother's sake.

NAT—[*Struggling.*] Did I say I had? Why do you look at me—like that?

SUE—Nat! Nat! For our mother's sake!

NAT—[*In terror.*] Stop! Stop! She's dead—

and at peace. Would you bring her tired soul back
to him again to be bruised and wounded?

Sue—Nat!

Nat—[*Clutching at his throat as though to
strangle something within him—hoarsely.*] Sue!
Have mercy! [*His sister stares at him with dread
foreboding.* Nat *calms himself with an effort and
continues deliberately:*] Smith said he would give
two thousand cash if I would sell the place to him
—and he would let me stay, rent free, as caretaker.

Sue—[*Scornfully.*] Two thousand! Why, over
and above the mortgage its worth——

Nat—It's not what it's worth. It's what one can
get, cash—for my book—for freedom!

Sue—So that's why he wants Father sent away,
the wretch! He must know the will Father made——

Nat—Gives the place to me. Yes, he knows. I
told him.

Sue—[*Dully.*] Ah, how vile men are!

Nat—[*Persuasively.*] If it were to be done—if
it were, I say—there'd be half for you for your
wedding portion. That's fair.

Sue—[*Horrified.*] Blood money! Do you think
I could touch it?

Nat—[*Persuasively.*] It would be only fair. I'd
give it you.

Sue—My God, Nat, are you trying to bribe me?

Nat—No. It's yours in all fairness. [*With a*

twisted smile.] You forget I'm heir to the treasure, too, and can afford to be generous. Ha-ha.

Sue—[*Alarmed.*] Nat! You're so strange. You're sick, Nat. You couldn't talk this way if you were yourself. Oh, we must go away from here —you and father and I! Let Smith foreclose. There'll be something over the mortgage; and we'll move to some little house—by the sea so that father——

Nat—[*Fiercely.*] Can keep up his mad game with me—whispering dreams in my ear—pointing out to sea—mocking me with stuff like this! [*He takes the bracelet from his pocket. The sight of it infuriates him and he hurls it into a corner, exclaiming in a terrible voice:*] No! No! It's too late for dreams now. It's too late! I've put them behind me to-night—forever!

Sue—[*Looks at him and suddenly understands that what she dreads has come to pass—letting her head fall on her outstretched arms with a long moan.*] Then—you've done it! You've sold him! Oh, Nat, you're cursed!

Nat—[*With a terrified glance at the roof above.*] Ssshh! What are you saying? He'll be better off —away from the sea.

Sue—[*Dully.*] You've sold him.

Nat—[*Wildly.*] No! No! [*He takes the map from his pocket.*] Listen, Sue! For God's sake, listen to me! See! The map of the island. [*He spreads it out on the table.*] And the treasure—where the cross is made. [*He gulps and his words pour out incoherently.*] I've carried it about for years. Is that nothing? You don't know what it means. It stands between me and my book. It's stood between me and life—driving me mad! *He* taught me to wait and hope with him—wait and hope—day after day. He made me doubt my brain and give the lie to my eyes—when hope was dead—when I knew it was all a dream—I couldn't kill it! [*His eyes starting from his head.*] God forgive me, I still believe! And that's mad—mad, do you hear?

Sue—[*Looking at him with horror.*] And that is why—you hate him!

Nat—No, I don't—— [*Then in a sudden frenzy.*] Yes! I do hate him! He's stolen my brain! I've got to free myself, can't you see, from him—and his madness.

Sue—[*Terrified—appealingly.*] Nat! Don't! You talk as if——

Nat—[*With a wild laugh.*] As if I were mad? You're right—but I'll be mad no more! See! [*He opens the lantern and sets fire to the map in his hand. When he shuts the lantern again it flickers and goes out. They watch the paper burn with fascinated eyes as he talks.*] See how I free myself and become sane. And now for facts, as the doctor said. I lied to you about him. He was a doctor from the asylum. See how it burns! It must all be destroyed—this poisonous madness. Yes, I lied to you—see—it's gone—the last speck—and the only other map is the one Silas Horne took to the bottom of the sea with him. [*He lets the ash fall to the floor and crushes it with his foot.*] Gone! I'm free of it—at last! [*His face is very pale, but he goes on calmly.*] Yes, I sold him, if you will—to save my soul. They're coming from the asylum to get him—— [*There is a loud, muffled cry from above, which sounds like "Sail-ho," and a stamping of feet. The slide to the companionway above is slid back with a bang. A gust of air tears down into the room.* NAT *and* SUE *have jumped to their feet and stand petrified.* CAPTAIN BARTLETT *tramps down the stairs.*]

NAT—[*With a shudder.*] God! Did he hear?

SUE—Ssshh! [CAPTAIN BARTLETT *comes into the room. He bears a striking resemblance to his son, but his face is more stern and formidable, his form more robust, erect and muscular. His mass of hair is pure white, his bristly mustache the same, contrasting with the weather-beaten leather color of his furrowed face. Bushy gray brows overhang the obsessed glare of his fierce dark eyes. He wears a heavy, double-breasted blue coat, pants of the same material, and rubber boots turned down from the knee.*]

BARTLETT—[*In a state of mad exultation strides toward his son and points an accusing finger at him.*

NAT *shrinks backward a step.*] Bin thinkin' me mad, did ye? Thinkin' it for the past three years, ye bin—ever since them fools on the Slocum tattled their damn lie o' the Mary Allen bein' a wreck.

NAT—[*Swallowing hard—chokingly.*] No—Father—I——

BARTLETT—Don't lie, ye whelp! You that I'd made my heir—aimin' to git me out o' the way! Aimin' to put me behind the bars o' the jail for mad folk!

SUE—Father—no!

BARTLETT—[*Waving his hand for her to be silent.*] Not you, girl, not you. You're your mother.

NAT—[*Very pale.*] Father—do you think—I——

BARTLETT—[*Fiercely.*] A lie in your eyes! I bin a-readin' 'em. My curse on you!

SUE—Father! Don't!

BARTLETT—Leave me be, girl. He believed, didn't he? And ain't he turned traitor—mockin' at me and sayin' it's all a lie—mockin' at himself, too, for bein' a fool to believe in dreams, as he calls 'em.

NAT—[*Placatingly.*] You're wrong, Father. I do believe.

BARTLETT—[*Triumphantly.*] Aye, now ye do! Who wouldn't credit their own eyes?

NAT—[*Mystified.*] Eyes?

BARTLETT—Have ye not seen her, then? Did ye not hear me hail?

NAT—[*Confusedly.*] Hail? I heard a shout. But—hail what?—seen what?

BARTLETT—[*Grimly.*] Aye, now's your punishment, Judas. [*Explosively.*] The Mary Allen, ye blind fool, come back from the Southern Seas—come back as I swore she must!

SUE—[*Trying to soothe him.*] Father! Be quiet. It's nothing.

BARTLETT—[*Not heeding her—his eyes fixed hypnotically on his son's.*] Turned the pint a half-hour back—the Mary Allen—loaded with gold as I swore she would be—carryin' her lowers—not a reef in 'em—makin' port, boy, as I swore she must—too late for traitors, boy, too late!—droppin' her anchor just when I hailed her.

NAT—[*A haunted, fascinated look in his eyes, which are fixed immovably on his father's.*] The Mary Allen! But how do you know?

BARTLETT—Not know my own ship! 'Tis you 're mad!

NAT—But at night—some other schooner——

BARTLETT—No other, I say! The Mary Allen—clear in the moonlight. And heed this: D'you call to mind the signal I gave to Silas Horne if he made this port o' a night?

NAT—[*Slowly.*] A red and a green light at the mainmast-head.

BARTLETT—[*Triumphantly.*] Then look out if ye dare! [*He goes to the porthole, left forward.*] Ye can see it plain from here. [*Commandingly.*] Will ye believe your eyes? Look—and then call me mad! [NAT *peers through the porthole and starts back, a dumbfounded expression on his face.*]

NAT—[*Slowly.*] A red and a green at the main-mast-head. Yes—clear as day.

SUE—[*With a worried look at him.*] Let me see. [*She goes to the porthole.*]

BARTLETT—[*To his son with fierce satisfaction.*] Aye, ye see now clear enough—too late for you. [NAT *stares at him spellbound.*] And from above I saw Horne and Cates and Jimmy Kanaka plain on the deck in the moonlight lookin' up at me. Come! [*He strides to the companionway, followed by* NAT. *The two of them ascend.* SUE *turns from the port-hole, an expression of frightened bewilderment on her face. She shakes her head sadly. A loud "Mary Allen, ahoy!" comes from above in* BART-LETT'S *voice, followed like an echo by the same hail from* NAT. SUE *covers her face with her hands, shuddering.* NAT *comes down the companionway, his eyes wild and exulting.*]

SUE—[*Brokenly.*] He's bad to-night, Nat. You're right to humor him. It's the best thing.

NAT—[*Savagely.*] Humor him? What in hell do you mean?

SUE—[*Pointing to the porthole.*] There's nothing there, Nat. There's not a ship in harbor.

NAT—You're a fool—or blind! The Mary Allen's there in plain sight of any one, with the red and the green signal lights. Those fools lied about her being wrecked. And I've been a fool, too.

SUE—But, Nat, there's nothing. [*She goes over to the porthole again.*] Not a ship. See.

NAT—I saw, I tell you! From above it's all plain. [*He turns from her and goes back to his seat by the table. SUE follows him, pleading frightenedly.*]

SUE—Nat! You mustn't let this—— You're all excited and trembling, Nat. [*She puts a soothing hand on his forehead.*]

NAT—[*Pushing her away from him roughly.*] You blind fool! [*Bartlett comes down the steps of the companionway. His face is transfigured with the ecstasy of a dream come true.*]

BARTLETT—They've lowered a boat—the three— Horne and Cates and Jimmy Kanaka. They're a-rowin' ashore. I heard the oars in the locks. Listen! [*A pause.*]

NAT—[*Excitedly.*] I hear!

SUE—[*Who has taken the chair by her brother— in a warning whisper.*] It's the wind and sea you hear, Nat. Please!

BARTLETT—[*Suddenly.*] Hark! They've landed. They're back on earth again as I swore they'd come

back. They'll be a-comin' up the path now. [*He
stands in an attitude of rigid attention.* NAT
*strains forward in his chair. The sound of the wind
and sea suddenly ceases and there is a heavy silence.
A dense green glow floods slowly in rhythmic waves
like a liquid into the room—as of great depths of
the sea faintly penetrated by light.*]

NAT—[*Catching at his sister's hand—chokingly.*]
See how the light changes! Green and gold! [*He
shivers.*] Deep under the sea! I've been drowned
for years! [*Hysterically.*] Save me! Save me!

SUE—[*Patting his hand comfortingly.*] Only
the moonlight, Nat. It hasn't changed. Be quiet,
dear, it's nothing. [*The green light grows deeper
and deeper.*]

BARTLETT—[*In a crooning, monotonous tone.*]
They move slowly—slowly. They're heavy, I know,
heavy—the two chests. Hark! They're below at
the door. You hear?

NAT—[*Starting to his feet.*] I hear! I left the
door open.

BARTLETT—For them?

NAT—For them.

SUE—[*Shuddering.*] Ssshh! [*The sound of a
door being heavily slammed is heard from way down
in the house.*]

NAT—[*To his sister—excitedly.*] There! You
hear?

Sue—A shutter in the wind.

Nat—There is no wind.

Bartlett—Up they come! Up, bullies! They're heavy—heavy! [*The paddling of bare feet sounds from the floor below—then comes up the stairs.*]

Nat—You hear them now?

Sue—Only the rats running about. It's nothing, Nat.

Bartlett—[*Rushing to the door and throwing it open.*] Come in, lads, come in!—and welcome home! [*The forms of* Silas Horne, Cates, *and* Jimmy Kanaka *rise noiselessly into the room from the stairs. The last two carry heavy inlaid chests.* Horne *is a parrot-nosed, angular old man dressed in gray cotton trousers and a singlet torn open across his hairy chest.* Jimmy *is a tall, sinewy, bronzed young Kanaka. He wears only a breech cloth.* Cates *is squat and stout and is dressed in dungaree pants and a shredded white sailor's blouse, stained with iron rust. All are in their bare feet. Water drips from their soaked and rotten clothes. Their hair is matted, intertwined with slimy strands of seaweed. Their eyes, as they glide silently into the room, stare frightfully wide at nothing. Their flesh in the green light has the suggestion of decomposition. Their bodies sway limply, nervelessly, rhythmically as if to the pulse of long swells of the deep sea.*]

NAT—[*Making a step toward them.*] See! [*Frenziedly.*] Welcome home, boys!

SUE—[*Grabbing his arm.*] Sit down, Nat. It's nothing. There's no one there. Father—sit down!

BARTLETT—[*Grinning at the three and putting his finger to his lips.*] Not here, boys, not here—not before him. [*He points to his son.*] He has no right, now. Come. The treasure is ours only. We'll go away with it together. Come. [*He goes to the companionway. The three follow. At the foot of it* HORNE *puts a swaying hand on his shoulder and with the other holds out a piece of paper to him.* BARTLETT *takes it and chuckles exultantly.*] That's right—for him—that's right! [*He ascends. The figures sway up after him.*]

NAT—[*Frenziedly.*] Wait! [*He struggles toward the companionway.*]

SUE—[*Trying to hold him back.*] Nat—don't! Father—come back!

NAT—Father! [*He flings her away from him and rushes up the companionway. He pounds against the slide, which seems to have been shut down on him.*]

SUE—[*Hysterically—runs wildly to the door in rear.*] Help! Help! [*As she gets to the door* DOCTOR HIGGINS *appears, hurrying up the stairs.*]

HIGGINS—[*Excitedly.*] Just a moment, Miss. What's the matter?

SUE—[*With a gasp.*] My father—up there!

HIGGINS—I can't see—where's my flash? Ah.
[*He flashes it on her terror-stricken face, then
quickly around the room. The green glow disappears. The wind and sea are heard again. Clear
moonlight floods through the portholes.* HIGGINS
springs to the companionway. NAT *is still pound-
ing.*] Here, Bartlett. Let me try.

NAT—[*Coming down—looking dully at the doctor.*] They've locked it. I can't get up.

HIGGINS—[*Looks up—in an astonished voice.*]
What's the matter, Bartlett? It's all open. [*He
starts to ascend.*]

NAT—[*In a voice of warning.*] Look out, man!
Look out for them!

HIGGINS—[*Calls down from above.*] Them?
Who? There's no one here. [*Suddenly—in alarm.*]
Come up! Lend a hand here! He's fainted!
[NAT *goes up slowly.* SUE *goes over and lights
the lantern, then hurries back to the foot of the
companionway with it. There is a scuffling noise
from above. They reappear, carrying* CAPTAIN
BARTLETT's *body.*]

HIGGINS—Easy now! [*They lay him on the
couch in rear.* SUE *sets the lantern down by the
couch.* HIGGINS *bends and listens for a heart-beat.
Then he rises, shaking his head.*] I'm sorry——

SUE—[*Dully.*] Dead?

HIGGINS—[*Nodding.*] Heart failure, I should

judge. [*With an attempt at consolation.*] Perhaps it's better so, if——

NAT—[*As if in a trance.*] There was something Horne handed him. Did you see?

SUE—[*Wringing her hands.*] Oh, Nat, be still! He's dead. [*To* HIGGINS *with pitiful appeal.*] Please go—go——

HIGGINS—There's nothing I can do?

SUE—Go—please—— [HIGGINS *bows stiffly and goes out.* NAT *moves slowly to his father's body, as if attracted by some irresistible fascination.*]

NAT—Didn't you see? Horne handed him something.

SUE—[*Sobbing.*] Nat! Nat! Come away! Don't touch him, Nat! Come away. [*But her brother does not heed her. His gaze is fixed on his father's right hand, which hangs downward over the side of the couch. He pounces on it and forcing the clenched fingers open with a great effort, secures a crumpled ball of paper.*]

NAT—[*Flourishing it above his head with a shout of triumph.*] See! [*He bends down and spreads it out in the light of the lantern.* The map of the island! Look! It isn't lost for me after all! There's still a chance—*my* chance! [*With mad, solemn decision.*] When the house is sold I'll go—and I'll find it! Look! It's written here in his hand writing: "The treasure is buried where the cross is made."

Sue—[*Covering her face with her hands—* brokenly.] Oh, God! Come away, Nat! Come away!

[*The Curtain Falls*]

THE ROPE

A Play In One Act

CHARACTERS

ABRAHAM BENTLEY
ANNIE, *his daughter*
PAT SWEENEY, *her husband*
MARY, *their child*
LUKE BENTLEY, *Abe's son by a second marriage*

THE ROPE

SCENE—*The interior of an old barn situated on top of a high headland of the seacoast. In the rear, to the left, a stall in which lumber is stacked up. To the right of it, an open double doorway looking out over the ocean. Outside the doorway, the faint trace of what was once a road leading to the barn. Beyond the road, the edge of a cliff which rises sheer from the sea below. On the right of the doorway, three stalls with mangers and hay-ricks. The first of these is used as a woodbin and is half full of piled-up cordwood. Near this bin, a chopping block with an ax driven into the top of it.*

The left section of the barn contains the hay loft, which extends at a height of about twelve feet from the floor as far to the right as the middle of the doorway. The loft is bare except for a few scattered mounds of dank-looking hay. From the edge of the loft, half way from the door, a rope about five feet long with an open running noose at the end is hanging.

*A rusty plow and various other farming imple-
ments, all giving evidence of long disuse, are
lying on the floor near the left wall. Farther
forward an old cane-bottomed chair is set back
against the wall.*

*In front of the stalls on the right stands a
long, roughly constructed carpenter's table, evidently home-made. Saws, a lathe, a hammer,
chisel, a keg containing nails and other tools
of the carpentry trade are on the table. Two
benches are placed, one in front, one to the
left of it.*

The right side of the barn is a bare wall.

*It is between six and half-past in the evening
of a day in early spring. At the rising of the
curtain some trailing clouds near the horizon,
seen through the open doorway, are faintly
tinged with gold by the first glow of the sunset.
As the action progresses this reflected light
gradually becomes brighter, and then slowly
fades into a smoky crimson. The sea is a
dark slate color. From the rocks below the
headland sounds the muffled monotone of breaking waves.*

As the curtain rises MARY *is discovered
squatting cross-legged on the floor, her back
propped against the right side of the doorway,
her face in profile. She is a skinny, over-grown*

girl of ten with thin, carroty hair worn in a pig-tail. She wears a shabby gingham dress. Her face is stupidly expressionless. Her hands flutter about aimlessly in relaxed, flabby gestures.

She is staring fixedly at a rag doll which she has propped up against the doorway opposite her. She hums shrilly to herself.

At a sudden noise from outside she jumps to her feet, peeks out, and quickly snatches up the doll, which she hugs fiercely to her breast. Then, after a second's fearful hesitation, she runs to the carpenter's table and crawls under it.

As she does so ABRAHAM BENTLEY *appears in the doorway and stands, blinking into the shadowy barn. He is a tall, lean stoop-shouldered old man of sixty-five. His thin legs, twisted by rheumatism, totter feebly under him as he shuffles slowly along by the aid of a thick cane. His face is gaunt, chalky-white, furrowed with wrinkles, surmounted by a shiny bald scalp fringed with scanty wisps of white hair. His eyes peer weakly from beneath bushy, black brows. His mouth is a sunken line drawn in under his large, beak-like nose. A two weeks' growth of stubby patches of beard covers his jaws and chin. He has on a threadbare brown overcoat but wears no hat.*

BENTLEY—[*Comes slowly into the barn, peering around him suspiciously. As he reaches the table and leans one hand on it for support,* MARY *darts from underneath and dashes out through the doorway.* BENTLEY *is startled; then shakes his cane after her.*] Out o' my sight, you Papist brat! Spawn o' Satan! Spyin' on me! They set her to it. Spyin' to watch me! [*He limps to the door and looks out cautiously. Satisfied, he turns back into the barn.*] Spyin' to see—what they'll never know. [*He stands staring up at the rope and taps it testingly several times with his stick, talking to himself as he does so.*] It's tied strong—strong as death—— [*He cackles with satisfaction.*] They'll see, then! They'll see! [*He laboriously creeps over to the bench and sits down wearily. He looks toward the sea and his voice quavers in a doleful chant:*] "Woe unto us! for the day goeth away, for the shadows of the evening are stretched out." [*He mumbles to himself for a moment—then speaks clearly.*] Spyin' on me! Spawn o' the Pit! [*He renews his chant.*] "They hunt our steps that we cannot go in our streets: our end is near, our days are fulfilled; for our end is come."

[*As he finishes* ANNIE *enters. She is a thin, slovenly, worn-out looking woman of about forty with a drawn, pasty face. Her habitual expression is one of a dulled irritation. She talks in a high-*

pitched, sing-song whine. She wears a faded ging-
ham dress and a torn sunbonnet.]

ANNIE—[*Comes over to her father but warily
keeps out of range of his stick.*] Paw! [*He doesn't
answer or appear to see her.*] Paw! You ain't
fergittin' what the doctor told you when he was
here last, be you? He said you was to keep still
and not go a-walkin' round. Come on back to the
house, Paw. It's gittin' near supper time and you
got to take your medecine b'fore it, like he says.

BENTLEY—[*His eyes fixed in front of him.*]
"The punishment of thine iniquity is accomplished,
O daughter of Zion: he will visit thine iniquity, O
daughter of Edom; he will discover thy sins."

ANNIE—[*Waiting resignedly until he has finished—wearily.*] You better take watch on your
health, Paw, and not be sneakin' up to this barn
no more. Lord sakes, soon 's ever my back is turned
you goes sneakin' off agen. It's enough to drive a
body outa their right mind.

BENTLEY—"Behold, every one that useth prov-
erbs shall use this proverb against thee, saying, As
is the mother, so is her daughter!" [*He cackles to
himself.*] So is her daughter!

ANNIE—[*Her face flushing with anger.*] And if
I am, I'm glad I take after her and not you, y'old
wizard! [*Scornfully.*] A fine one you be to be
shoutin' Scripture in a body's ears all the live-long
day—you that druv Maw to her death with your

naggin', and pinchin', and miser stinginess. If you've a mind to pray, it's down in the medder you ought to go, and kneel down by her grave, and ask God to forgive you for the meanness you done to her all her life.

BENTLEY—[*Mumbling.*] "As is the mother, so is her daughter."

ANNIE—[*Enraged by the repetition of this quotation.*] *You* quotin' Scripture! Why, Maw wasn't cold in the earth b'fore you was down in the port courtin' agen—courtin' that harlot that was the talk o' the whole town! And then you disgraces yourself and me by marryin' her—*her*—and bringin' her back home with you; and me still goin' every day to put flowers on Maw's grave that you'd fergotten. [*She glares at him vindictively, pausing for breath.*] And between you you'd have druv me into the grave like you done Maw if I hadn't married Pat Sweeney so's I could git away and live in peace. Then you took on so high and mighty 'cause he was a Cath'lic—*you* gittin' religion all of a moment just for spite on me 'cause I'd left—and b'cause she egged you on against me; *you* sayin' it was a sin to marry a Papist, after not bein' at Sunday meetin' yourself for more'n twenty years!

BENTLEY—[*Loudly.*] "He will visit thin iniquity——"

ANNIE—[*Interrupting.*] And the carryin's-on you had the six years at home after I'd left you—

the shame of the whole county! Your wife, indeed, with a child she *claimed* was your'n, and her goin' with this farmer and that, and even men off the ships in the port, and you blind to it! And then when she got sick of you and ran away—only to meet her end at the hands of God a year after— she leaves you alone with that—*your* son, Luke, *she* called him—and him only five years old!

Bentley—[*Babbling.*] Luke? Luke?

Annie—[*Tauntingly.*] Yes, Luke! "As is the mother, so is her son"—that's what you ought to preach 'stead of puttin' curses on me. You was glad enough to git me back home agen, and Pat with me, to tend the place, and help bring up that brat of hers. [*Jealously.*] You was fond enough of him all them years—and how did he pay you back? Stoie your money and ran off and left you just when he was sixteen and old enough to help. Told you to your face he'd stolen and was leavin'. He only laughed when you was took crazy and cursed him; and he only laughed harder when you hung up that silly rope there [*She points.*] and told him to hang himself on it when he ever came home agen.

Bentley—[*Mumbling.*] You'll see, then. You'll see!

Annie—[*Wearily—her face becoming dull and emotionless again.*] I s'pose I'm a bigger fool than you be to argy with a half-witted body. But I tell you agen that Luke of yours ain't comin' back; and if he does he ain't the kind to hang himself, more's the pity. He's like her. He'd hang *you* more likely if he s'pected you had any money. So you might 's well take down that ugly rope you've had tied there since he run off. He's probably dead anyway by this.

BENTLEY—[*Frightened.*] No! No!

ANNIE—Them as bad as him comes to a sudden end. [*Irritably.*] Land sakes, Paw, here I am argyin' with your lunatic notions and the supper not ready. Come on and git your medicine. You can see no one ain't touched your old rope. Come on! You can sit 'n' read your Bible. [*He makes no movement. She comes closer to him and peers into his face—uncertainly.*] Don't you hear me? I do hope you ain't off in one of your fits when you don't know nobody. D'you know who's talkin'? This is Annie—your Annie, Paw.

BENTLEY—[*Bursting into senile rage.*] None o' mine! Spawn o' the Pit! [*With a quick movement he hits her viciously over the arm with his stick. She gives a cry of pain and backs away from him, holding her arm.*]

ANNIE—[*Weeping angrily.*] That's what I git for tryin' to be kind to you, you ugly old devil! [*The sound of a man's footsteps is heard from outside, and* SWEENEY *enters. He is a stocky, muscular, sandy-haired Irishman dressed in patched cordu-*

*roy trousers shoved down into high laced boots, and
a blue flannel shirt.   The bony face of his bullet
head has a pressed-in appearance except for his
heavy jaw, which sticks out pugnaciously.   There
is an expression of mean cunning and cupidity about
his mouth and his small, round, blue eyes.   He has
evidently been drinking and his face is flushed and
set in an angry scowl.*]

SWEENEY—Have ye no supper at all made, ye
lazy slut?   [*Seeing that she has been crying.*]
What're you blubberin' about?

ANNIE—It's all his fault.   I was tryin' to git him
home but he's that set I couldn't budge him; and
he hit me on the arm with his cane when I went near
him.

SWEENEY—He did, did he?   I'll soon learn him
better.   [*He advances toward* BENTLEY *threateningly.*]

ANNIE—[*Grasping his arm.*]   Don't touch him,
Pat.   He's in one of his fits and you might kill him.

SWEENEY—An' good riddance!

BENTLEY—[*Hissing.*]   Papist!   [*Chants.*]   "Pour
out thy fury upon the heathen that know thee not,
and upon the families that call not on thy name: for
they have eaten up Jacob, and devoured him, and
consumed him, and made his habitation desolate."

SWEENEY—[*Instinctively crosses himself—then
scornfully.*]   Spit curses on me till ye choke.   It's
not likely the Lord God'll be listenin' to a wicked

auld sinner the like of you. [*To* ANNIE.] What's got into him to be roamin' up here? When I left for the town he looked too weak to lift a foot.

ANNIE—Oh, it's the same crazy notion he's had ever since Luke left. He wanted to make sure the rope was still here.

BENTLEY—[*Pointing to the rope with his stick.*] He-he! Luke'll come back. Then you'll see. You'll see!

SWEENEY—[*Nervously.*] Stop that mad cacklin' for the love of heaven! [*With a forced laugh.*] It's great laughter I should be havin' at you, mad as you are, for thinkin' that thief of a son of yours would come back to hang himself on account of your curses. It's five years he's been gone, and not a sight of him; an' you, cursin' an' callin' down the wrath o' God on him by day an' by night. That shows you what God thinks of your curses—an' Him deaf to you!

ANNIE—It's no use talkin' to him, Pat.

SWEENEY—I've small doubt but that Luke is hung long since—by the police. He's come to no good end, that lad. [*His eyes on the rope.*] I'll be pullin' that thing down, so I will; an' the auld loon'll stay in the house, where he belongs, then, maybe. [*He reaches up for the rope as if to try and yank it down. BENTLEY waves his stick frantically in the air, and groans with rage.*]

ANNIE—[*Frightened.*] Leave it alone, Pat.

Look at him. He's liable to hurt himself. Leave his rope be. It don't do no harm.

SWEENEY—[*Reluctantly moves away.*] It looks ugly hangin' there open like a mouth. [*The old man sinks back into a relieved immobility.* SWEENEY *speaks to his wife in a low tone.*] Where's the child? Get her to take him out o' this. I want a word with you he'll not be hearin'. [*She goes to the door and calls out:*] Ma-ry! Ma-ry! [*A faint, answering cry is heard and a moment later* MARY *rushes breathlessly into the barn.* SWEENEY *grabs her roughly by the arm. She shrinks away, looking at him with terrified eyes.*] You're to take your grandfather back to the house—an' see to it he stays there.

ANNIE—And give him his medicine.

SWEENEY—[*As the child continues to stare at him silently with eyes stupid from fear, he shakes her impatiently.*] D'you hear me, now? [*To his wife.*] It's soft-minded she is, like I've always told you, an' stupid; and you're not too firm in the head yourself at times, God help you! An' look at him! It's the curse is in the wits of your family, not mine.

ANNIE—You've been drinkin' in town or you wouldn't talk that way.

MARY—[*Whining.*] Maw! I'm skeered!

SWEENEY—[*Lets go of her arm and approaches* BENTLEY.] Get up out o' this, ye auld loon, an'

go with Mary. She'll take you to the house.
[BENTLEY *tries to hit him with the cane.*] Oho, ye
would, would ye? [*He wrests the cane from the old
man's hands.*] Bad cess to ye, you're the treach-
'rous one! Get up, now! [*He jerks the old man
to his feet.*] Here, Mary, take his hand. Quick
now! [*She does so tremblingly.*] Lead him to the
house.

ANNIE—Go on, Paw! I'll come and git your
supper in a minute.

BENTLEY—[*Stands stubbornly and begins to in-
tone.*] "O Lord, thou hast seen my wrong; judge
thou my cause. Thou hast seen all their vengeance
and all their imaginations against me——"

SWEENEY—[*Pushing him toward the door.
BENTLEY tries to resist. MARY pulls at his hand in
a sudden fit of impish glee, and laughs shrilly.*] Get
on now an' stop your cursin'.

BENTLEY—"Render unto them a recompense, O
Lord, according to the work of their hands."

SWEENEY—Shut your loud quackin'! Here's
your cane. [*He gives it to the old man as they
come to the doorway and quickly steps back out of
reach.*] An' mind you don't touch the child with it
or I'll beat you to a jelly, old as ye are.

BENTLEY—[*Resisting MARY's efforts to pull him
out, stands shaking his stick at SWEENEY and his
wife.*] "Give them sorrow of heart, thy curse unto

them. Persecute and destroy them in anger from under the heavens of the Lord."

MARY—[*Tugging at his hand and bursting again into shrill laughter.*] Come on, gran'paw. [*He allows himself to be led off, right.*]

SWEENEY—[*Making the sign of the cross furtively—with a sigh of relief.*] He's gone, thank God! What a snake's tongue he has in him! [*He sits down on the bench to the left of table.*] Come here, Annie, till I speak to you. [*She sits down on the bench in front of table.* SWEENEY *winks mysteriously.*] Well, I saw him, sure enough.

ANNIE—[*Stupidly.*] Who?

SWEENEY—[*Sharply.*] Who? Who but Dick Waller, the lawyer, that I went to see. [*Lowering his voice.*] An' I've found out what we was wishin' to know. [*With a laugh.*] Ye said I'd been drinkin'—which is true; but 'twas all in the plan I'd made. I've a head for strong drink, as ye know, but he hasn't. [*He winks cunningly.*] An' the whiskey loosened his tongue till he'd told all he knew.

ANNIE—He told you—about Paw's will?

SWEENEY—He did. [*Disappointedly.*] But for all the good it does us we might as well be no wiser than we was before. [*He broods for a moment in silence—then hits the table furiously with his fist.*] God's curse on the auld miser!

ANNIE—What did he tell you?

SWEENEY—Not much at the first. He's a cute

one, an' he'd be askin' a fee to tell you your own name, if he could get it. His practice is all dribbled away from him lately on account of the drink. So I let on I was only payin' a friendly call, havin' known him for years. Then I asked him out to have a drop o' drink, knowin' his weakness; an' we had rashers of them, an' I payin' for it. Then I come out with it straight and asked him about the will—because the auld man was crazy an' on his last legs, I told him, an' he was the lawyer made out the will when Luke was gone. So he winked at me an' grinned—he was drunk by this—an' said: "It's no use, Pat. He left the farm to the boy." "To hell with the farm," I spoke back. "It's mortgaged to the teeth; but how about the money?" "The money?" an' he looks at me in surprise, "What money?" "The cash he has," I says. "You're crazy," he says. "There wasn't any cash—only the farm." "D'you mean to say he made no mention of money in his will?" I asked. You could have knocked me down with a feather. "He did not—on my oath," he says. [SWEENEY *leans over to his wife—indignantly.*] Now what d'you make o' that? The auld divil!

ANNIE—Maybe Waller was lyin'.

SWEENEY—He was not. I could tell by his face. He was surprised to hear me talkin' of money.

ANNIE—But the thousand dollars Paw got for the mortgage just before that woman ran away——

Sweeney—An' that I've been slavin' me hands off to pay the int'rist on!

Annie—What could he have done with that? He ain't spent it. It was in twenty dollar gold pieces he got it, I remember Mr. Kellar of the bank tellin' me once.

Sweeney—Divil a penny he's spent. Ye know as well as I do if it wasn't for my hammerin', an' sawin', an' nailin', he'd be in the poor house this minute—or the mad house, more likely.

Annie—D'you suppose that harlot ran off with it?

Sweeney—I do not; I know better—an' so do you. D'you not remember the letter she wrote tellin' him he :ould support Luke on the money he'd got on the mortgage she'd signed with him; for he'd made the farm over to her when he married her. An' where d'you suppose Luke got the hundred dollars he stole? The auld loon must have had cash with him then, an' it's only five years back.

Annie—He's got it hid some place in the house most likely.

Sweeney—Maybe you're right. I'll dig in the cellar this night when he's sleepin'. He used to be down there a lot recitin' Scripture in his fits.

Annie—What else did Waller say?

Sweeney—Nothin' much; except that we should put notices in the papers for Luke, an' if he didn't come back by sivin years from when he'd left—two

years from now, that'd be—the courts would say
he was dead an' give us the farm.   Divil a lot of use
it is to us now with no money to fix it up; an' himself ruinin' it years ago by sellin' everythin' to buy
that slut new clothes.

ANNIE—Don't folks break wills like his'n in the
courts?

SWEENEY—Waller said 'twas no use.   The auld
divil was plain in his full senses when he made it;
an' the courts cost money.

ANNIE—[*Resignedly.*]   There ain't nothin' we
can do then.

SWEENEY—No—except wait an' pray that young
thief is dead an' won't come back; an' try an' find
where it is the auld man has the gold hid, if he has
it yet.   I'd take him by the neck an' choke him till
he told it, if he wasn't your father.   [*He takes a
full quart flask of whiskey from the pocket of his
coat and has a big drink.*]   Aahh!   If we'd on'y
the thousand we'd stock the farm good an' I'd give up
this dog's game [*He indicates the carpentry outfit
scornfully.*] an' we'd both work hard with a man
or two to help, an' in a few years we'd be rich; for
'twas always a payin' place in the auld days.

ANNIE—Yes, yes, it was always a good farm
then.

SWEENEY—He'll not last long in his senses, the
doctor told me.   His next attack will be very soon
an' after it he'll be a real lunatic with no legal

claims to anythin'. If we on'y had the money——
'Twould be the divil an' all if the auld fool should
forget where he put it, an' him takin' leave of his
senses altogether. [*He takes another nip at the
bottle and puts it back in his pocket—with a sigh.*]
Ah, well, I'll save what I can an' at the end of two
years, with good luck in the trade, maybe we'll have
enough. [*They are both startled by the heavy footsteps of some one approaching outside. A shrill
burst of* MARY's *laughter can be heard and the deep
voice of a man talking to her.*]

SWEENEY—[*Uneasily.*] It's Mary; but who
could that be with her? It's not himself. [*As he
finishes speaking* LUKE *appears in the doorway, holding the dancing* MARY *by the hand. He is a tall,
strapping young fellow about twenty-five with a
coarse-featured, rather handsome face bronzed by
the sun. What his face lacks in intelligence is
partly forgiven for his good-natured, half-foolish
grin, his hearty laugh, his curly dark hair, a certain
devil-may-care recklessness and irresponsible youth
in voice and gesture. But his mouth is weak
and characterless; his brown eyes are large
but shifty and acquisitive. He wears a dark blue
jersey, patched blue pants, rough sailor shoes, and
a gray cap. He advances into the stable with a
mocking smile on his lips until he stands directly
under the rope. The man and woman stare at him
in petrified amazement.*]

Annie—Luke!

Sweeney—[*Crossing himself.*] Glory be to God —it's him!

Mary—[*Hopping up and down wildly.*] It's Uncle Luke, Uncle Luke, Uncle Luke! [*She runs to her mother, who pushes her away angrily.*]

Luke—[*Regarding them both with an amused grin.*] Sure, it's Luke—back after five years of bummin' round the rotten old earth in ships and things. Paid off a week ago—had a bust-up—and then took a notion to come out here—bummed my way—and here I am. And you're both of you tickled to death to see me, ain't yuh?—like hell! [*He laughs and walks over to* Annie.] Don't yuh even want to shake flippers with your dear, long-lost brother, Annie? I remember you and me used to git on so fine together—like hell!

Annie—[*Giving him a venomous look of hatred.*] Keep your hands to yourself.

Luke—[*Grinning.*] You ain't changed, that's sure—on'y yuh're homlier'n ever. [*He turns to the scowling Sweeney.*] How about you, brother Pat?

Sweeney—I'd not lower myself to take the hand of a——

Luke—[*With a threat in his voice.*] Easy goes with that talk! I'm not so soft to lick as I was when I was a kid; and don't forget it.

Annie—[*To* Mary, *who is playing catch with a silver dollar which she has had clutched in her hand—sharply.*] Mary! What have you got there? Where did you get it? Bring it here to me this minute! [MARY *presses the dollar to her breast and remains standing by the doorway in stubborn silence.*]

LUKE—Aw, let her alone! What's bitin' yuh? That's on'y a silver dollar I give her when I met her front of the house. She told me you was up here; and I give her that as a present to buy candy with. I got it in Frisco—cart-wheels, they call 'em. There ain't none of them in these parts I ever seen, so I brung it along on the voyage.

ANNIE—[*Angrily.*] I don't know or care where you got it—but I know you ain't come by it honest. Mary! Give that back to him this instant! [*As the child hesitates, she stamps her foot furiously.*] D'you hear me? [MARY *starts to cry softly, but comes to* LUKE *and hands him the dollar.*]

LUKE—[*Taking it—with a look of disgust at his half-sister.*] I was right when I said you ain't changed, Annie. You're as stinkin' mean as ever. [*To* MARY, *consolingly.*] Quit bawlin', kid. You 'n' me'll go out on the edge of the cliff here and chuck some stones in the ocean same's we useter, remember? [MARY'S *tears immediately cease. She looks up at him with shining eyes, and claps her hands.*]

MARY—[*Pointing to the dollar he has in his hand.*] Throw that! It's flat 'n' it'll skip.

Luke—[*With a grin.*] That's the talk, kid. That's all it's good for—to throw away; not buryin' it like your miser folks'd tell you. Here! You take it and chuck it away. It's your'n. [*He gives her the dollar and she hops to the doorway. He turns to* Pat *with a grin.*] I'm learnin' your kid to be a sport, Tight-Wad. I hope you ain't got no objections.

Mary—[*Impatiently.*] Come on, Uncle Luke. Watch me throw it.

Luke—Aw right. [*To* Pat.] I'll step outside a second and give you two a chanct to git all the dirty things yuh're thinkin' about me off your chest. [*Threateningly.*] And then I'm gointer come and talk turkey to you, see? I didn't come back here for fun, and the sooner you gets that in your beans, the better.

Mary—Come on and watch me!

Luke—Aw right, I'm comin'. [*He walks out and stands, leaning his back against the doorway, left.* Mary *is about six feet beyond him on the other side of the road. She is leaning down, peering over the edge of the cliff and laughing excitedly.*]

Mary—Can I throw it now? Can I?

Luke—Don't git too near the edge, kid. The water's deep down there, and you'd be a drowned rat if you slipped. [*She shrinks back a step.*] You chuck it when I say three. Ready, now! [*She draws back her arm.*] One! Two! Three!

[*She throws the dollar away and bends down to see it hit the water.*]

MARY—[*Clapping her hands and laughing.*] I seen it! I seen it splash! It's deep down now, ain't it?

LUKE—Yuh betcher it is! Now watch how far I kin chuck rocks. [*He picks up a couple and goes to where she is standing. During the following conversation between* SWEENEY *and his wife he continues to play this way with* MARY. *Their voices can be heard but the words are indistinguishable.*]

SWEENEY—[*Glancing apprehensively toward the door—with a great sigh.*] Speak of the divil an' here he is! [*Furiously.*] Flingin' away dollars, the dirty thief, an' us without——

ANNIE—[*Interrupting him.*] Did you hear what he said? A thief like him ain't come back for no good. [*Lowering her voice.*] D'you s'pose he knows about the farm bein' left to him?

SWEENEY—[*Uneasily.*] How could he? An' yet—I dunno—[*With sudden decision.*] You'd best lave him to me to watch out for. It's small sense you have to hide your hate from him. You're as looney as the rist of your breed. An' he needs to be blarneyed round to fool him an' find out what he's wantin'. I'll pritind to make friends with him, God roast his soul! An' do you run to the house an' break the news to the auld man; for if he seen him suddin its likely the little wits he has left would leave him; an' the thief could take the farm from us to-morrow if himself turned a lunatic.

ANNIE—[*Getting up.*] I'll tell him a little at a time till he knows.

SWEENEY—Be careful, now, or we'll lose the farm this night. [*She starts towards the doorway.* SWEENEY *speaks suddenly in a strange, awed voice.*] Did you see Luke when he first came in to us? He stood there with the noose of the rope almost touchin' his head. I was almost wishin'—— [*He hesitates.*]

ANNIE—[*Viciously.*] I was wishin' it was round his neck chokin' him, that's what I was—hangin' him just as Paw says.

SWEENEY—Ssshh! He might hear ye. Go along, now. He's comin' back.

MARY—[*Pulling at* LUKE'S *arm as he comes back to the doorway.*] Lemme throw 'nother! Lemme throw 'nother!

LUKE—[*Enters just as* ANNIE *is going out and stops her.*] Goin' to the house? Do we get any supper? I'm hungry.

ANNIE—[*Glaring at him but restraining her rage.*] Yes.

LUKE—[*Jovially.*] Good work! And tell the old man I'm here and I'll see him in a while. He'll be glad to see me, too—like hell! [*He comes forward.* ANNIE *goes off, right.*]

MARY—[*In an angry whine, tugging at his hand.*]
Lemme throw 'nother. Lemme——

LUKE—[*Shaking her away.*] There's lots of
rocks, kid. Throw them. Dollars ain't so plenti-
ful.

MARY—[*Screaming.*] No! No! I don' wanter
throw rocks. Lemme throw 'nother o' them.

SWEENEY—[*Severely.*] Let your uncle in peace,
ye brat! [*She commences to cry.*] Run help your
mother now or I'll give ye a good hidin'. [MARY
runs out of the door, whimpering. PAT *turns to*
LUKE *and holds out his hand.*]

LUKE—[*Looking at it in amazement.*] Ahoy,
there! What's this?

SWEENEY—[*With an ingratiating smile.*] Let's
let by-gones be by-gones. I'm harborin' no grudge
agen you these past years. Ye was only a lad when
ye ran away an' not to be blamed for it. I'd have
taken your hand a while back, an' glad to, but for
her bein' with us. She has the divil's own tongue,
as ye know, an' she can't forget the rowin' you an'
her used to be havin'.

LUKE—[*Still looking at* SWEENEY's *hand.*] So
that's how the wind blows! [*With a grin.*] Well,
I'll take a chanct. [*They shake hands and sit down
by the table,* SWEENEY *on the front bench and* LUKE
on the left one.]

SWEENEY—[*Pulls the bottle from his coat pocket*

—with a wink.] Will ye have a taste? It's real stuff.

LUKE—Yuh betcher I will! [*He takes a big gulp and hands the bottle back.*]

SWEENEY—[*After taking a drink himself, puts bottle on table.*] I wasn't wishin' herself to see it or I'd have asked ye sooner. [*There is a pause, during which each measures the other with his eyes.*]

LUKE—Say, how's the old man now?

SWEENEY—[*Cautiously.*] Oh, the same as ivir—older an' uglier, maybe.

LUKE—I thought he might be in the bug-house by this time.

SWEENEY—[*Hastily.*] Indeed not; he's foxy to pritind he's looney, but he's his wits with him all the time.

LUKE—[*Insinuatingly.*] Is he as stingy with his coin as he used to be?

SWEENEY—If he owned the ocean he wouldn't give a fish a drink; but I doubt if he's any money left at all. Your mother got rid of it all, I'm thinkin'. [LUKE *smiles a superior, knowing smile.*] He has on'y the farm, an' that mortgaged. I've been payin' the int'rist an' supportin' himself an' his doctor's bills by the carpentryin' these five years past.

LUKE—[*With a grin.*] Huh! Yuh're slow. Yuh oughter get wise to yourself.

SWEENEY—[*Inquisitively.*] What d'ye mean by that?

Luke—[*Aggravatingly.*] Aw, nothin'. [*He turns around and his eyes fix themselves on the rope.*] What the hell—— [*He is suddenly convulsed with laughter and slaps his thigh.*] Hahaha! If that don't beat the Dutch! The old nut!

Sweeny—What?

Luke—That rope. Say, has he had that hangin' there ever since I skipped?

Sweeney—[*Smiling.*] Sure; an' he thinks you'll be comin' home to hang yourself.

Luke—Hahaha! Not this chicken! And you say he ain't crazy! Gee, that's too good to keep. I got to have a drink on that. [Sweeney *pushes the bottle toward him. He raises it toward the rope.*] Here's how, old chum! [*He drinks.* Sweeney *does likewise.*] Say, I'd a'most forgotten about that. Remember how hot he was that day when he hung that rope up and cussed me for pinchin' the hundred? He was standin' there shakin' his stick at me, and I was laughin' 'cause he looked so funny with the spit dribblin' outa his mouth like he was a mad dog. And when I turned round and beat it he shouted after me: "Remember, when you come home again there's a rope waitin' for yuh to hang yourself on, yuh bastard!" [*He spits contemptuously.*] What a swell chanct. [*His manner changes and he frowns.*] The old slave-driver! That's a hell of a fine old man for a guy to have!

Sweeney—[*Pushing the bottle toward him.*]

Take a sup an' forgit it. 'Twas a long time past.

Luke—But the rope's there yet, ain't it? And he keeps it there. [*He takes a large swallow. Sweeney also drinks.*] But I'll git back at him aw right, yuh wait 'n' see. I'll git every cent he's got this time.

Sweeney—[*Slyly.*] If he has a cent. I'm not wishful to discourage ye, but—— [*He shakes his head doubtfully, at the same time fixing Luke with a keen glance out of the corner of his eye.*]

Luke—[*With a cunning wink.*] Aw, he's got it aw right. You watch me! [*He is beginning to show the effects of the drink he has had. He pulls out tobacco and a paper and rolls a cigarette and lights it. As he puffs he continues boastfully.*] You country jays oughter wake up and see what's goin' on. Look at me. I was green as grass when I left here, but bummin' round the world, and bein' in cities, and meetin' all kinds, and keepin' your two eyes open—that's what'll learn yuh a cute trick or two.

Sweeney—No doubt but you're right. Us country folks is stupid in most ways. We've no chance to learn the things a travelin' lad like you'd be knowin'.

Luke—[*Complacently.*] Well, you watch me and I'll learn yuh. [*He snickers.*] So yuh think the ʼld man's flat broke, do yuh?

Sweeney—I do so.

Luke—Then yuh're simple; that's what—simple!
You're lettin' him kid yuh.

Sweeney—If he has any, it's well hid, I know
that. He's a sly old bird.

Luke—And I'm a slyer bird. D'yuh hear that?
I c'n beat his game any time. You watch me! [*He
reaches out his hand for the bottle. They both drink
again.* Sweeney *begins to show signs of getting
drunk. He hiccoughs every now and then and his
voice grows uncertain and husky.*]

Sweeney—It'd be a crafty one who'd find where
he'd hidden it, sure enough.

Luke—You watch me! I'll find it. I betcher
anything yuh like I find it. You watch me! Just
wait till he's asleep and I'll show yuh—ter-night.
[*There is a noise of shuffling footsteps outside and*
Annie's *whining voice raised in angry protest.*]

Sweeney—Ssshh! It's himself comin' now. [Luke
*rises to his feet and stands, waiting in a defensive at-
titude, a surly expression on his face. A moment later*
Bentley *appears in the doorway, followed by* Annie. *He leans against the wall, in an extraordinary
state of excitement, shaking all over, gasping for
breath, his eyes devouring* Luke *from head to foot.*]

Annie—I couldn't do nothin' with him. When I
told him *he'd* come back there was no holdin' him.
He was a'most frothin' at the mouth till I let him
out. [*Whiningly.*] You got to see to him, Pat, if
you want any supper. I can't——

SWEENEY—Shut your mouth! We'll look after him.

ANNIE—See that you do. I'm goin' back. [*She goes off, right.* LUKE *and his father stand looking at each other. The surly expression disappears from* LUKE's *face, which gradually expands in a broad grin.*]

LUKE—[*Jovially.*] Hello, old sport! I s'pose yuh're tickled to pieces to see me—like hell! [*The old man stutters and stammers incoherently as if the very intensity of his desire for speech had paralyzed all power of articulation.* LUKE *turns to Pat.*] I see he ain't lost the old stick. Many a crack on the nut I used to get with that.

BENTLEY—[*Suddenly finding his voice—chants.*] "Bring forth the best robe, and put it on him; and put a ring on his hand, and shoes on his feet: And bring hither the fatted calf, and kill it; and let us eat, and be merry: For this my son was dead, and is alive again; he was lost, and is found." [*He ends up with a convulsive sob.*]

LUKE—[*Disapprovingly.*] Yuh're still spoutin' the rotten old Word o' God same's ever, eh? Say, give us a rest on that stuff, will yuh? Come on and shake hands like a good sport. [*He holds out his hand. The old man totters over to him, stretching out a trembling hand.* LUKE *seizes it and pumps it up and down.*] That's the boy!

SWEENEY—[*Genuinely amazed.*] Look at that,

would ye—the two-faced auld liar. [BENTLEY *passes his trembling hand all over* LUKE, *feeling of his arms, his chest, his back. An expression of overwhelming joy suffuses his worn features.*]

LUKE—[*Grinning at* SWEENEY.] Say, watch this. [*With tolerant good-humor.*] On the level I b'lieve the old boy's glad to see me at that. He looks like he was tryin' to grin; and I never seen him grin in my life, I c'n remember. [*As* BENTLEY *attempts to feel of his face.*] Hey, cut it out! [*He pushes his hand away, but not roughly.*] I'm all here, yuh needn't worry. Yuh needn't be scared I'm a ghost. Come on and sit down before yuh fall down. Yuh ain't got your sea-legs workin' right. [*He guides the old man to the bench at left of table.*] Squat here for a spell and git your wind. [BENTLEY *sinks down on the bench.* LUKE *reaches for the bottle.*] Have a drink to my makin' port. It'll buck yuh up.

SWEENEY—[*Alarmed.*] Be careful, Luke. It might likely end him.

LUKE—[*Holds the bottle up to the old man's mouth, supporting his head with the other hand.* BENTLEY *gulps, the whiskey drips over his chin, and he goes into a fit of convulsive coughing.* LUKE *laughs.*] Hahaha! Went down the wrong way, did it? I'll show yuh the way to do it. [*He drinks.*] There yuh are—smooth as silk. [*He hands the bottle to* SWEENEY, *who drinks and puts it back on the table.*]

Sweeney—He must be glad to see ye or he'd not drink. 'Tis dead against it he's been these five years past. [*Shaking his head.*] An' him cursin' you day an' night! I can't put head or tail to it. Look out he ain't meanin' some bad to ye underneath. He's crafty at pretendin'.

Luke—[*As the old man makes signs to him with his hand.*] What's he after now? He's lettin' on he's lost his voice again. What d'yuh want? [Bentley *points with his stick to the rope. His lips move convulsively as he makes a tremendous effort to utter words.*]

Bentley—[*Mumbling incoherently.*] Luke—Luke—rope—Luke—hang.

Sweeney—[*Appalled.*] There ye are! What did I tell you? It's to see you hang yourself he's wishin', the auld fiend!

Bentley—[*Nodding.*] Yes—Luke—hang.

Luke—[*Taking it as a joke—with a loud guffaw.*] Hahaha! If that don't beat the Dutch! The old nanny-goat! Aw right, old sport. Anything to oblige. Hahaha! [*He takes the chair from left and places it under the rope. The old man watches him with eager eyes and seems to be trying to smile. Luke stands on the chair.*]

Sweeney—Have a care, now! I'd not be foolin' with it in your place.

Luke—All out for the big hangin' of Luke Bentley by hisself. [*He puts the noose about his neck with an air of drunken bravado and grins at his father. The latter makes violent motions for him to go on.*] Look at him, Pat. By God, ne's in a hurry. Hahaha! Well, old sport. here goes nothin'. [*He makes a movement as if he were going to jump and kick the chair from under him.*]

SWEENEY—[*Half starts to his feet—horrified.*] Luke! Are ye gone mad?

LUKE—[*Stands staring at his father, who is still making gestures for him to jump. A scowl slowly replaces his good-natured grin.*] D'yuh really mean it—that yuh want to see me hangin' myself? [BENT-LEY *nods vigorously in the affirmative.* LUKE *glares at him for a moment in silence.*] Well, I'll be damned! [*To Pat.*] An' I thought he was only kiddin'. [*He removes the rope gingerly from his neck. The old man stamps his foot and gesticulates wildly, groaning with disappointment.* LUKE *jumps to the floor and looks at his father for a second. Then his face grows white with a vicious fury.*] I'll fix your hash, you stinkin' old murderer! [*He grabs the chair by its back and swings it over his head as if he were going to crush* BENTLEY'S *skull with it. The old man cowers on the bench in abject terror.*]

SWEENEY—[*Jumping to his feet with a cry of alarm.*] Luke! For the love of God! [LUKE *hesitates; then hurls the chair in back of him under the loft, and stands menacingly in front of his father, his hands on his hips.*]

LUKE—[*Grabbing* BENTLEY'S *shoulder and shaking him—hoarsely.*] Yuh wanted to see me hangin' there in real earnest, didn't yuh? You'd hang me yourself if yuh could, wouldn't yuh? And you my own father! Yuh damned son of a gun! Yuh would, would yuh? I'd smash your brains out for a nickel! [*He shakes the old man more and more furiously.*]

SWEENEY—Luke! Look out! You'll be killin' him next.

LUKE—[*Giving his father one more shake, which sends him sprawling on the floor.*] Git outa here! Git outa this b'fore I kill yuh dead! [SWEENEY *rushes over and picks the terrified old man up.*] Take him outa here, Pat! [*His voice rises to a threatening roar.*] Take him outa here or I'll break every bone in his body! [*He raises his clenched fists over his head in a frenzy of rage.*]

SWEENEY—Ssshh! Don't be roarin'! I've got him. [*He steers the whimpering, hysterical* BENTLEY *to the doorway.*] Come out o' this, now. Get down to the house! Hurry now! Ye've made enough trouble for one night. [*They disappear off right.* LUKE *flings himself on a bench, breathing heavily. He picks up the bottle and takes a long swallow.* SWEENEY *reënters from rear. He comes over and sits down in his old place.*] Thank God he's off down to the house, scurryin' like a frightened hare as if he'd never a kink in his legs in his life. He was moanin' out loud so you could hear him a long

ways. [*With a sigh.*] It's a murd'rous auld loon
he is, sure enough.

LUKE—[*Thickly.*] The damned son of a gun!

SWEENEY—I thought you'd be killin' him that
time with the chair.

LUKE—[*Violently.*] Serve him damn right if I
done it.

SWEENEY—An' you laughin' at him a moment
sooner! I thought 'twas jokin' ye was.

LUKE—[*Sullenly.*] So I was kiddin'; but I
thought he was tryin' to kid me, too. And then I
seen by the way he acted he really meant it. [*Banging the table with his fist.*] Ain't that a hell of a
fine old man for yuh!

SWEENEY—He's a mean auld swine.

LUKE—He meant it aw right, too. Yuh shoulda
seen him lookin' at me. [*With sudden lugubrious-
ness.*] Ain't he a hell of a nice old man for a guy
to have? Ain't he?

SWEENEY—[*Soothingly.*] Hush! It's all over
now. Don't be thinkin' about it.

LUKE—[*On the verge of drunken tears.*] How
kin I help thinkin'—and him my own father? After
me bummin' and starvin' round the rotten earth, and
workin' myself to death on ships and things—and
when I come home he tries to make me bump off—
wants to see me a corpse—my own father, too! Ain't
he a hell of an old man to have? The rotten son
of a gun!

SWEENEY—It's past an' done. Forgit it. [*He slaps* LUKE *on the shoulder and pushes the bottle toward him.*] Let's take a drop more. We'll be goin' to supper soon.

LUKE—[*Takes a big drink—huskily.*] Thanks. [*He wipes his mouth on his sleeve with a snuffle.*] But I'll tell yuh something you can put in your pipe and smoke. It ain't past and done, and it ain't goin' to be! [*More and more aggressively.*] And I ain't goin' to ferget it, either! Yuh kin betcher life on that, pal. And *he* ain't goin' to ferget it—not if he lives a million—not by a damned sight! [*With sudden fury.*] I'll fix his hash! I'll git even with him, the old skunk! You watch me! And this very night, too!

SWEENEY—How d'you mean?

LUKE—You just watch me, I tell yuh! [*Banging the table.*] I said I'd git even and I will git even— this same night, with no long waits, either! [*Frowning.*] Say, you don't stand up for him, do yuh?

SWEENEY—[*Spitting—vehemently.*] That's child's talk. There's not a day passed I've not wished him in his grave.

LUKE [*Excitedly.*] Then we'll both git even on him—you 'n' me. We're pals, ain't we?

SWEENEY—Sure.

LUKE—And yuh kin have half what we gits. That's the kinda feller I am! That's fair enough, ain't it?

SWEENEY—Surely.

LUKE—I don't want no truck with this rotten farm. You kin have my share of that. I ain't made to be no damned dirt puncher—not me! And I ain't goin' to loaf round here more'n I got to, and when I goes this time I ain't never comin' back. Not me! Not to punch dirt and milk cows. You kin have the rotten farm for all of me. What I wants is cash—regular coin yuh kin spend—not dirt. I want to show the gang a real time, and then ship away to sea agen or go bummin' agen. I want coin yuh kin throw away—same's your kid chucked that dollar of mine overboard, remember? A real dollar, too! She's a sport, aw right!

SWEENEY—[*Anxious to bring him back to the subject.*] But where d'you think to find his money?

LUKE—[*Confidently.*] Don't yuh fret. I'll show yuh. You watch me! I know his hidin' places. I useter spy on him when I was a kid—— Maw used to make me—and I seen him many a time at his sneakin'. [*Indignantly.*] He used to hide stuff from the old lady. What d'yuh know about him—the mean skunk.

SWEENEY—That was a long time back. You don't know——

LUKE—[*Assertively.*] But I do know, see! He's got two places. One was where I swiped the hundred.

SWEENEY—It'll not be there, then.

Luke—No; but there's the other place; and he never knew I was wise to that. I'd have left him clean on'y I was a kid and scared to pinch more. So you watch me! We'll git even on him, you 'n' me, and go halfs, and yuh kin start the rotten farm goin' agen and I'll beat it where there's some life.

Sweeney—But if there's no money in that place, what'll you be doin' to find out where it is, then?

Luke—Then you 'n' me 'ull make him tell!

Sweeney—Oho, don't think it! 'Tis not him'd be tellin'.

Luke—Aw, say, you're simple! You watch me! I know a trick or two about makin' people tell what they don't wanter. [*He picks up the chisel from the table.*] Yuh see this? Well, if he don't answer up nice and easy we'll show him! [*A ferocious grin settles over his face.*] We'll git even on him, you 'n' me—and he'll tell where it's hid. We'll just shove this into the stove till it's red hot and take off his shoes and socks and warm the bottoms of his feet for him. [*Savagely.*] He'll tell then—anything we wants him to tell.

Sweeney—But Annie?

Luke—We'll shove a rag in her mouth so's she can't yell. That's easy.

Sweeney—[*His head lolling drunkenly—with a cruel leer.*] 'Twill serve him right to heat up his hoofs for him, the limpin', auld miser!—if ye don't hurt him too much.

LUKE—[*With a savage scowl.*] We won't hurt him—more'n enough. [*Suddenly raging.*] I'll pay him back aw right! He won't want no more people to hang themselves when I git through with him. I'll fix his hash! [*He sways to his feet, the chisel in his hand.*] Come on! Let's git to work. Sooner we starts the sooner we're rich. [SWEENEY *rises. He is steadier on his feet than* LUKE. *At this moment* MARY *appears in the doorway.*]

MARY—Maw says supper's ready. I had mine. [*She comes into the room and jumps up, trying to grab hold of the rope.*] Lift me, Uncle Luke. I wanter swing.

LUKE—[*Severely.*] Don't yuh dare touch that rope, d'yuh hear?

MARY—[*Whining.*] I wanter swing.

LUKE—[*With a shiver.*] It's bad, kid. Yuh leave it alone, take it from me.

SWEENEY—She'll get a good whalin' if I catch her jumpin' at it.

LUKE—Come on, pal. T'hell with supper. We got work to do first. [*They go to the doorway.*]

SWEENEY—[*Turning back to the sulking Mary.*] And you stay here, d'you hear, ye brat, till we call ye—or I'll skin ye alive.

LUKE—And ter-morrer mornin', kid, I'll give yuh a whole handful of them shiny, bright things yuh chucked in the ocean—and yuh kin be a real sport.

MARY—[*Eagerly.*] Gimme 'em now! Gimme 'em now, Uncle Luke. [*As he shakes his head—whiningly.*] Gimme one! Gimme one!

LUKE—Can't be done, kid. Ter-morrer. Me 'n' your old man is goin' to git even now—goin' to make him pay for——

SWEENEY—[*Interrupting—harshly.*] Hist with your noise! D'you think she's no ears? Don't be talkin' so much. Come on, now.

LUKE—[*Permitting himself to be pulled out the doorway.*] Aw right! I'm with yuh. We'll git even—you 'n' me. The damned son of a gun! [*They lurch off to the right.*]

[MARY *skips to the doorway and peeps after them for a moment. Then she comes back to the center of the floor and looks around her with an air of decision. She sees the chair in under the loft and runs over to it, pulling it back and setting it on its legs directly underneath the noose of the rope. She climbs and stands on the top of the chair and grasps the noose with both her upstretched hands. Then with a shriek of delight she kicks the chair from under her and launches herself for a swing. The rope seems to part where it is fixed to the beam. A dirty gray bag tied to the end of the rope falls to the floor with a muffled, metallic thud. MARY sprawls forward on her hands and knees, whimpering. Straggly wisps from the pile of rank hay fall silently to the floor in a mist of dust. MARY, discovering she is un-*

hurt, glances quickly around and sees the bag. She pushes herself along the floor and, untying the string at the top, puts in her hand. She gives an exclamation of joy at what she feels and, turning the bag upside down, pours its contents in her lap. Giggling to herself, she gets to her feet and goes to the doorway, where she dumps what she has in her lap in a heap on the floor just inside the barn. They lie there in a little glittering pile, shimmering in the faint sunset glow—fifty twenty-dollar gold pieces. MARY *claps her hands and sings to herself:* "Skip— skip—skip." *Then she quickly picks up four or five of them and runs out to the edge of the cliff. She throws them one after another into the ocean as fast as she can and bends over to see them hit the water. Against the background of horizon clouds still tinted with blurred crimson she hops up and down in a sort of grotesque dance, clapping her hands and laughing shrilly. After the last one is thrown she rushes back into the barn to get more.]*

MARY—[*Picking up a handful—giggling ecstatically.*] Skip! Skip! [*She turns and runs out to throw them as*

[*The Curtain Falls*]